CW00642908

"I require anyone who works on my commercial teams to read one book on selling... this one!"

Cary G. Vance, *General Manager, Sales, GE Healthcare*

"Thanks to the content in Dan's book, we have witnessed incredible metamorphoses within our team. His Trust Triangle Selling approach has translated to immediate sales for our team. His tools are simple and easy to implement immediately."

Jay D. Miller, *President and CEO, Vital Images, Inc.*

"Adams's unique, process-based approach to guiding customers makes *Building Trust, Growing Sales* a must read for anyone wishing to call themselves a sales professional. It simplifies the complex!"

Craig Schiefelbein, *President and CEO, Paragon Development Systems, Inc.*

"If you are selling expensive software, complex solutions, or technology, you must read this book. Well written and well organized, it outlines a new and highly consultative approach to working with customers."

Lawrence S. Dolin, *Chairman, President, and CEO, Noteworthy Medical Systems, Inc.*

"As a sales executive with more than twenty-five years of both direct sales and sales management experience, I have had the opportunity to read many how-to books. *Building Trust, Growing Sales* offers a direct and clear message that will quickly pay significant dividends to any sales organization. Dan Adams's message and sales training tools — and now this book — are helping to shape our sales culture and develop our sales teams into true sales professionals."

Steven P. Canakes, *Executive Vice President, Global Sales, Vital Images, Inc.*

BUILDING TRUST
GROWING SALES

BUILDING TRUST
GROWING SALES

How to master
complex, high-end sales
using the principles of
Trust Triangle Selling™

BY DANIEL J. ADAMS

Trust Triangle™, Trust Triangle Selling™, Objection Vaporizer™, and Prospecting Machine™ are trademarks of Adams & Associates, 532 Walker Road, Hinsdale, Illinois 60521. www.trusttriangleselling.com

The example companies, organizations, products, domain names, e-mail addresses, logos, people, places, and events depicted herein are fictitious. No association with any real company, organization, product, domain name, e-mail address, logo, person, place, or event is intended or should be inferred.

Published by Balagot Communications, Inc., Chicago, Illinois. www.balagotcommunications.com

Book design and production by Arc Group Ltd., Chicago, Illinois. www.arcgroupltd.com

ISBN 0-9786069-0-6

Library of Congress Control Number: 2006926561

First Edition

Manufactured in the United States of America

To my wife, Mary, whose unwavering love, support, and encouragement during the tumultuous ups and downs of a long selling career have made this book possible. Convincing her to say yes to my marriage proposal represents the most important sale I ever made.

ACKNOWLEDGMENTS

A special thank you to those who provided assistance in writing this book. With immense gratitude to these magnificent people for their support, ideas, hard work, creativity, encouragement, proofreading, editing, artistry, inspiration, and more:

Alice Adams	Michael Chiodi	Samuel O'Rear
Edward Adams	Thomas D'Amico	Amy Peltonen
Mary Adams	Michael Hills	Jeffrey Rains
Robert Adams	Blake Johnson	Marvin Slosman
Brian Battey	Joen Kinnan	Matthew Suggs
Peter Casey	Gregory Matre	

…and to the thousands of customers, colleagues, and clients who have had a huge impact on this book by evidencing their trust in me during my sales career, sharing their stories, and joining me in my training workshops.

…and to our editor extraordinaire, Maija Rothenberg. Conscious of my literary weaknesses, I realized that hiring the right editor for this book was imperative. All the editors I interviewed were brightly starred, highly recommended, and experienced. Most, however, responded with the standard, "My fee is X dollars per word." Only one shined immediately as a true and natural consultant. She took it upon herself to review parts of my manuscript, offering up observations and revised copy – no charge, no obligation. Just honest interest in my project. Maija immersed herself in sales theories, completely absorbed consultative selling concepts, and truly humanized my manuscript. She is an amazing individual and professional. Thank you, Maija.

TABLE OF CONTENTS

Secret Weapons

FOREWORD

I first heard about Dan when I joined GE Healthcare. His reputation as a super salesman was legendary. People would say, "He never loses a deal," "His customers love him," "He knows more about the customers than they do!" Of course Dan always ranked at the top of the charts on performance and on commissions.

You can imagine my excitement when my manager said I would get to train with Dan. I would be able to learn from the man, the myth, and the legend himself! I had two weeks to absorb all the information I could.

When the time came, I was not disappointed. Dan was six foot three, two hundred ten pounds, and spoke with a radio announcer's voice. He looked permanent-pressed in his fine tailored suit — I was in the presence of greatness. I learned a great deal from Dan in those two weeks about sales and about business. He always had a plan. He was a student of the game. He was a phenomenal communicator. He studied his customers and knew their needs, wants, desires, families, favorite foods, sports, and hobbies. He knew his customers' "love language" — whether it was price or features or technology. He was a machine! Dan did nothing by accident.

One day during my training we stopped at one of Dan's accounts. I wish I could remember the name of the gentleman I talked with. Dan was leaving a "footprint" (business card) in another office, and I had an opportunity to speak with the customer alone. I used the time to ask his advice on how I could be successful in my new position. He pointed toward the door Dan had just exited and said,

"Study him!" The customer went on to explain that it wasn't just Dan's product knowledge or sales skills that impressed him – it was the total package. It was Dan's consultative approach and the way he took the time to build trust – not just by helping the customer solve problems but helping to avoid them altogether.

I did indeed study Dan, and I observed something else – his yearning to help. Dan's eagerness to share his thoughts, theories, and sales practices is genuine – and his enthusiasm for sales is contagious. Just as he openly and thoughtfully helped me over the course of my career, he offers the same generosity of spirit and expertise to readers picking up this book. You are in for a treat!

Brian Battey
Chief Operating Officer
International Physician Networks
Baltimore, Maryland

PREFACE

► Coaching by Fire ◄

My sales manager loomed over me. This was no small feat for Sam, given that he was six inches shorter than I was. Somehow he always managed to seem taller. Sam was potbellied and had a bad back that made him waddle when he walked. Still, he managed to intimidate me, a twenty-two-year-old fresh out of grad school.

He shook his head in exasperation and bewilderment. Four months into my yearlong training program at General Electric Healthcare, I was making every mistake in the book. The day before, out of frustration over his teaching philosophy, I had kicked a trash can across the room, making everyone in the office jump and sending debris clattering across the floor.

"Maybe you're not cut out for this, Dan," he said. "You might want to think about another line of work."

I went home that day feeling worthless. A total failure. I was a guy with an MBA, some selling experience, the right attitude (or so I thought), and a willingness to learn. Still, I could not figure it out. It was humiliating.

My previous mentors – my mom and dad, Bob and Alice Adams, and my basketball coach, Verne Luebstorf – had been kind, encouraging my self-confidence and building me up. Sam O'Rear's goal seemed to be to tear me down.

"He's turning you into an abused dog," my wife said. Mary didn't like Sam's penetrating gaze or the way he wouldn't let go of her hand the first time they shook. She didn't understand why I admired him and wanted to please him so much.

It was because Sam knew his stuff, I told her. He knew exactly how to conduct himself with customers and employees. I was convinced that he knew what it took to become a sales superstar. Despite my discomfort, I saw that his harshness was a means to an end. He was trying to motivate me to work harder to absorb his teachings. He wanted me to succeed, not fail.

So I decided to hang in. I wouldn't give up. Making mistakes was inevitable, I reasoned — but repeating them didn't need to be. I gave myself permission to make every kind of mistake possible — but only once.

When I showed up the next day, Sam's attitude had shifted. He flashed a big toothy grin; he knew he had me.

It got much better after that.

———◆———

A dozen years later, in recognition of outstanding achievement, I was setting records for the highest number of nominations to GE's President's Club for sales success.

I listened to Sam. I wrote things down. I paid attention to my higher-achieving colleagues. I analyzed what worked and what didn't. I created tools and shortcuts — my secret weapons — and gradually developed the methodology presented in this book.

By the time I left GE, my skill set and personality profile had been evaluated along with other superstars and had become the model for new GE hires. In a test measuring these traits (some of which we'll discuss in chapter 1), I achieved the highest score ever.

After GE I moved on to marketing and sales positions at Cisco Systems and then to Ariba, Inc. In September 2001, together with the rest of the world, Mary and I watched in horror at the events unfolding on our TV screen. Life suddenly felt very short. I realized that after pushing so hard for twenty-two years, I had finally accomplished everything I had wanted to accomplish. It was time to pull the plug. We decided to sell some of our stock and other holdings.

Mary and I hovered over the speakerphone on the call to Charles Schwab. We were shocked at the blasé attitude of the clerk who obeyed our order to sell. In a bored voice he recited the resulting seven-figure deposit to our account.

We hung up the phone and squealed. Then we jumped in our kayaks and toured the lake in disbelief. Bobbing on the lake, paddling away, I yelled into the wind. At the ripe old age of 42, I had achieved what some call critical mass — the freedom to do what I want, when I want. For me, it was personal and professional liberation!

▶ Goals of This Book ◀

I tell you my story not to boast — though I am proud of my accomplishments. I share it because I believe that you, too, can achieve superstar status in your industry — without making all the mistakes I did.

By following this methodology and using these tools, you can strengthen your selling skills and create long-term relationships with your customers while maintaining your credibility and integrity. It's a win-win equation: you win *with* your customers — not at their expense.

My methodology, Trust Triangle Selling, incorporates new, sophisticated consultative and strategic selling principles and integrates three processes: the Customer Decision Process (chapter 2), the Customer Buying Process (chapter 3), and the Superstar Selling Process (chapter 4).

The insights here apply to all sales situations; however, because of the sales trenches in which I toiled, these methods are particularly well suited to sales involving:

- ▶ High-risk transactions
- ▶ Big-ticket products, solutions, and services
- ▶ Educated customers
- ▶ The top officers of major organizations
- ▶ Complex buying processes
- ▶ Long sales cycles

I admire Sam's business skills and sales expertise, and I'm grateful for his generosity and wisdom. I still take issue, though, with some of his teaching methods. I have a lot of empathy for sales reps who are now experiencing the discomfort I went through before I finally got it. I'm committed to showing you the shortcuts — the most effective way to get from A to Z. (Why bother with the long route?) I offer this gathering of best practices as an easier, kinder way to learn — one that will save you time and spare you pain. Sam and my other mentors would call this "paying it forward" — offering a hand up to the next generation of sales professionals.

Good luck!

CHAPTER ONE

QUALITIES OF A SUPERSTAR

▶ What Kind of Sales Rep Are You? ◀

Let's imagine the following scenario.

You walk into a shoe store with your family to buy yourself a pair of shoes. Oscar, the sales rep, immediately approaches and asks, "Can I help you?" You pick out a pair of shoes, Oscar brings you the size you asked for, and you try them on.

"I don't think I like the shape of the toe box," you say.

"They look good on you, though," Oscar says.

"They feel a little snug."

"They'll stretch out," Oscar says. "That's top-quality leather. The best."

When you shop here, it is solely (so to speak) up to you to make sure you get a pair of shoes that fit well. Except for finding the correct shoebox in the back room, Oscar provides no help. He responds to your objections by denying they exist.

Oscar knows shoes, but rarely reveals his knowledge. He lets his customers buy shoes that slip at the heel or are not wide enough ("Hey – they should buy what they want!"), because he knows that even if the shoes don't work out and if they languish, unworn, in the customer's closet, only some customers will bother to return them.

He never hands out his business card or invites anyone to call with questions. That would only invite problems.

Oscar's focus is not on customer relations but on moving product: the more pairs of shoes he moves and the faster he moves them, the more he gets paid. He knows none of his customers' names — unless, perhaps, their checks bounce. He keeps no records of what customers buy. He calls no one to tell them about upcoming sales. The store has a coupon program to encourage repeat sales, but he does nothing beyond that to keep customers coming back.

Your experience of buying from Oscar was less than stellar. You got the shoes that you wanted at a not-outrageous price, but you got little else. Walking into the shoe store, seeing all the salespeople check you out, you felt like a goldfish surrounded by hungry cats. When you shop here again — and you probably will, because the store carries the brands of shoes you want — you won't seek out one sales rep over another, because they are all pretty much interchangeable.

Oscar is an old-school sales rep — and not a very good one at that. He's an order taker, not a consultant. His game is Harvest the Money, in which the customer is a combatant, not an ally. In short, he is interested in *selling* shoes, not in helping his customers *buy* shoes.

———◆———

Next door to the shoe store is a restaurant. Catharine, the manager and maître d', greets you warmly the moment you walk in. "How are you today?" she says, extending her hand. "Good to see you again." She shows you to your favorite table by the window and pulls out your chair for you. Standing by your table with her hands clasped behind her back, she inquires about your health and whether you got caught in the rainstorm. She tells you about today's specials and asks what you're in the mood for.

"If you'd like something light, I recommend the filet," she says. "Unless you're still watching your cholesterol. In that case I recommend the grilled chicken breast and tabbouleh."

Catharine is a font of information about all things food. She remembers that you are allergic to shellfish. She can tell you where to buy the freshest arugula and which pan to use when pan-searing salmon at home. She knows which brand of cooktop produces the highest heat. She's always willing to answer questions, and she never steers you wrong. She is your ally, not your combatant. Not only does she know her product, but — more important — she knows you.

After your meal, when she overhears you discussing Italian ice, which she doesn't serve in her restaurant, she recommends another restaurant a few blocks away. "Their Italian ices are good," she says with a wink. "But stay away from those cannolis."

Catharine follows a consultative style of selling — she puts even more emphasis on the customer relationship than she does on the products she markets — the food, ambience, and service of her restaurant. She is passionate about food, true — but the food itself is not the point. Making her customers happy is the point. The product she sells is only the medium by which she satisfies her customers. Many of her loyal customers would gladly follow her to any restaurant in the city.

Catharine knows that her customers can get *fed* anywhere: there are a thousand restaurants in her city. They come to her because they respect and trust her. They respect the standards she sets in her restaurant and trust that their dining experience will be positive, time and time again. If, for some reason, something goes wrong, Catharine will fix it.

★ **SUPERSTAR SECRET** ★

Don't sell. Consult!

When the holiday season rolls around, and your company casts about for a place to hold its annual party, whom do you call? Catharine, of course. When you need someone to cater your spouse's birthday party, she arranges for the food and waitstaff. You call her about everything. She provides something invisible over and above her party platters.

Catharine is not just a consultant — she's a superstar.

———◆———

Across the street from Catharine's restaurant is another superstar. As you enter Knopf's Clothing, Bill greets you by name, shakes your hand, and smiles. "You take a 44 long, not a regular," he says, showing off his memory. "Since you bought a grey jacket the last time you were in, you don't need another grey one now. How about I show you something in navy?"

Bill keeps your size and purchase information in his personal digital assistant, which he consults frequently. "I remember you didn't like the herringbone, so I'm going to show you a solid. And I have the perfect shirt for it." Bill quietly expands the product line horizons while anticipating your complete needs. You count on his impeccable taste and know that he, like Catharine, will never steer you wrong. If Bill were to move to a different store, you'd follow him there in a heartbeat.

———◆———

At this point in your sales career, are you more like Oscar? Or is your selling style closer to Catharine's and Bill's? There's an easy way I can test you without even observing you in action with a customer. I only need to ask this question. If I instructed you to pick up the phone right now and call a prospective customer, how would you feel? Does your gut say, "Oh, boy!" or "Oh, no!" If it says "oh, no," there could be a number of reasons for this, but I suspect it has to do with how you understand sales and therefore how you see yourself as a salesperson.

If you understand sales as talking people into buying things they don't need, overpowering customers with your persuasiveness, pushing facts and figures down their throats, backing people into a corner and jabbering them to death until they give in, or tricking them out of their hard-earned money, *of course* you don't want to pick up the phone! Why would anyone want to do *that* for a living? That's the old school of selling; no wonder you're resistant to calling.

On the other hand, if you think of sales as helping people solve their problems, offering your expertise to guide them through an unfamiliar process, preventing customers' headaches, establishing long-term relationships with customers, helping customers succeed, and receiving accolades not just for your product but for your knowledge and assistance, doesn't that sound more appealing? Seeing it that way makes you want to pick up the phone, doesn't it? When you're confident you have something of value to offer, you're naturally eager to share it. (If you're *not* confident about your product or service, you won't succeed. If you're working for a company that lacks credibility and trustworthiness, you won't be able to turn around and do good work for your customers. Your first and most important sale, as they say, is to yourself.)

> ### ★ SUPERSTAR SECRET ★
> **Superstar sales is not about selling. It's about helping people buy.**

Think of consultative sales as being the good guy, not the bad guy. You can trade in your black hat for a white one. You still work enormously hard, but with a different attitude and focus. You hold your head up high during the day and sleep with a clear conscience, because you are truly serving customers, not tricking them into buying something they neither want nor need.

▶ The Value of Your Knowledge ◀

Your ingrained beliefs about sales reps — and therefore yourself as a sales rep — will affect your success. If you see sales reps as vultures rather than helpers, you'll never get anywhere. One of my long-standing clients has been GE. I have coached thousands of GE technical sales reps on how to develop their selling skills. Typically, at first, the reps are reluctant to approach physicians. They are scared stiff, because they don't want to "sell." They don't want to be perceived as the stereotypical salesperson.

Superstar sales is not about selling. It's about helping people buy. It's not about pushing a product or solution — it's about guiding your customer through all the headaches involved in a major purchase. If you think sales is about selling, you'll never be able to walk up to customers. People don't want to be sold; you don't want to sell. But would you walk up to them to consult? You have a vast amount of experience and an ability to help these people, and if you look at approaching your customers as a way of *helping them,* not *selling to them,* then it will be much less intimidating to approach them. When you're not trying to convince them to give you money, when you approach them with a genuine desire to be of assistance, then the feelings of intimidation vanish.

It's intimidating to call a CEO if you want to sell her a $2 million CT (computed tomography) scanner. It's not intimidating to call a CEO if you can genuinely provide a 20% improvement in her hospital's net income by providing services and solutions that can improve the quality of patient care, increase the hospital's revenue or productivity, or decrease the hospital's costs. That's not intimidating – that's something you need to be talking with the CEO about.

What's getting in your way as a sales rep? It may be the natural good manners that you grew up with. You don't want to be a pain in the behind and you don't want to be perceived as a charity case. You don't want to ask for something for nothing. If you believe that approaching customers is intruding on their privacy, you will dig in your heels and it'll be hard to go forward. You're thinking, "I don't want to be a jerk!" But if you reframe the interaction to that of the helper, who is actually doing a service and providing something of value, then you square up your shoulders and hold your head up high.

▶ Becoming a True Consultant ◀

Understanding the value you bring to the table is only half of the consultative sales equation. There's another piece. Once you get your thinking straight, you don't just pick up the phone and call a customer. Part of being a superstar is having the humility to realize that you don't know enough about the customer yet to *really be a consultant.* First you have to do some research on that person and that company so that you can customize your services and intelligently articulate the value you can bring to them. Of course, this assumes that you actually *can* bring value to them. Superstars are open and honest if they cannot bring value. It would be the height of arrogance to call someone up and say, "I know what's good for you."

You need to understand the customer's needs or pains (or both) so that you can put your solution into customized terms that the customer will value. That means (1) researching the customer's needs (we'll talk about research in chapter 4), (2) listening to the customer directly, and (3) determining whether you can be of assistance Yes! In some circumstances you may have to tell your customer that you are not the right fit.

Inside the Sales Rep's Mind

Old School Rep

▶ How can I win this deal?

▶ What features should I highlight to prove we are best?

▶ What makes our product unique?

▶ What do I need to do to beat my competition?

▶ How can I sell my product?

Consultative Rep

▶ How can I help my customer be more successful?

▶ How can I help my customer be more competitive?

▶ How can I positively influence the financial health of my customer?

▶ How can I serve as a consultant to help my customer invest in my product?

I started out using the old-school way of thinking, feeling out of control and panicky. Too many reps are just reacting — they're frustrated and scared that they are not achieving. I had that same miserable feeling. At some point in my career, the lights turned on. It doesn't *have* to be that way! There's a much easier way, where everything goes smoothly and you and the customer jointly determine what pathway you want to walk down — and then walk down that pathway together. As a consultative sales rep you're no longer reacting and worrying that you don't know what's going on. You no longer feel jerked around by the customer — suddenly, you and the customer are allies, not opponents. Customers start calling you to seek your advice.

As a consultative rep, you're not selling widgets, you're helping customers find solutions to their problems. You're providing something invisible above and beyond the thing for which the dollars are exchanged. You bring knowledge to the table — valuable assistance.

If you truly get this, you'll have self-respect, which allows you to calm down. You'll have high self-esteem, because you know you're treating customers well and because you understand the value of what you're providing — even if some customers may choose not to take advantage of that.

Helping Customers Avoid Headaches

People don't buy products or services or features or benefits — they buy solutions to their problems and pain. Unfortunately, most marketing departments usually feed their sales reps only product information: "Here's how you plug it in and turn it on, here's how our product is different from competing products." The marketing people don't tell the reps what the product or service provides — benefits that will directly help solve the customer's problem.

Selling a CT scanner to a hospital (or selling any expensive, technical product or solution to a customer) serves as a good example. Look at the transaction from the buyer's standpoint. Imagine what it's like to be Dr. Alice Murphy, the Medical Director of Radiology, whose job it is to buy a CT. Think about the hassles that go along with the investment in a multimillion-dollar, high-tech piece of medical diagnostic equipment. Dr. Murphy feels overwhelmed with all the steps around the selection and installation of the CT, to say nothing of the training requirements. Hundreds of choices have to be made and dozens of processes carefully coordinated in order to make the project successful.

Dr. Murphy is facing myriad potential headaches. The trouble is, she's not aware of most of them and therefore doesn't understand their seriousness or how to avoid them. Because such purchases of high-ticket, high-tech equipment are so infrequent, many buyers go into it thinking, "Oh, it's simple. You just call someone up and buy it." The reality couldn't be farther from the truth.

It's incumbent upon the superstar to share with the customer ways to prevent headaches. And if the customer balks and says, "I don't really need you to assist me with project timetables, bid specifications, budgetary pricing, architectural plans, or room site preparations," ask yourself, "Why would a customer say this?" There could be several reasons: (1) He does not realize, or you have not convinced him, that headaches lie ahead; (2) he does not realize, or you have not convinced him, that you could help prevent or solve his headaches; or (3) you have not gained his trust.

If my customer balked, I would say, "Great. No problem. But just let me make you aware that if we *don't* do this, here are the headaches you may face down the road." That's a very powerful approach to making sure customers will allow you to guide them down the pathway — a mutually agreed upon pathway.

These are not scare tactics. You're not saying to the customer, "Buy my parachute or you're going to die." To make sure that that is clear, as soon as you encounter resistance (for example, the customer says, "No, I don't think we need your help with that"), you provide references. You tell the customer about another customer who was in a similar situation and who did not take the time to go through these steps. Then you share the resulting headaches.

> ★ **SUPERSTAR SECRET** ★
>
> **People don't buy products or services or features or benefits. They buy solutions to their problems and pain.**

Here are some examples of the headaches that a superstar rep would warn Dr. Murphy about and help her avoid:

- ▸ *Missed time schedules.* The hospital leadership has a plan to install a CT within a particular time frame. They're counting on a revenue stream from the project. They're starting to advertise this brand-new capability or upgrade. The marketing department is sending out brochures and notifying all the providers. An open house is planned to let all the surgeons know, so the hospital can start getting those referrals. The open house is the compelling event (see page 51) upon which the whole timetable depends. Imagine the consequences for Dr. Murphy if she misses that deadline. What if it's not ready when it's supposed to be ready?

▶ *Cost overruns.* These can occur for a million reasons, such as a contractor's forgetting to bring power to where it was needed.

▶ *Unhappy customers.* In the case of a hospital CT, the customers include the providers of care, surgeons, referring physicians, end-user customers (the patients), and the families of those end-user customers. The hospital doesn't want to harm any of these constituents; they all have to be kept happy.

▶ *Product does not fit the needs.* Dr. Murphy is focused on her specialty (radiology) and may not have the needs of the other specialties (surgery, oncology, orthopedics, and so on) high on her priority list. Because of this, she may have blinders on relative to the needs of other departments. She doesn't make these purchases often and is paid to be a radiologist — not a professional buyer. A superstar rep would recognize this and ensure that communication flows well throughout the hospital — by no means taking credit, but clearly acting as a funnel of solid, accurate information in an organization that is lacking this capability.

▶ *Product does not work.* Examples of this include frequent downtime, inadequate training of personnel, or the equipment's not being optimized for the type of patients the hospital serves. For instance, one U.S. hospital holds itself out as a leader in women's health care, but it purchased dead-end technology that cannot perform a new, nonsurgical uterine fibroid procedure called magnetic resonance–guided focused ultrasound.

▶ *Legal requirements not met.* An inexperienced buyer might not know about the state requirements regarding radiation protection, sanitary practices, and the handling and disposal of hazardous materials or the federal requirements around the Health Insurance Portability and Accountability Act of 1996 (HIPAA).

▶ *Facility problems.* These include inadequate air conditioning in a room housing heat-producing equipment. If the room has inadequate venting, Dr. Murphy will have a multimillion-dollar headache.

▶ *Poor layout.* Dr. Murphy has to consider the flow of patients coming in and out. Does she want one patient coming out the same door that another patient is entering? Throughput — the speed of transition from patient 1 to patient 2 — becomes very important to scheduling, as does how the physician enters and exits. Does he have to backtrack? If you were drawing up plans for a new house, would you put the kitchen right next to the front door? No, you'd design a greeting area near the entrance.

▶ *Future needs not taken into consideration.* The hospital leadership forgets to think about future needs because they don't have a pro helping them. A good example would be if the hospital wants two CT scanners. They put one in and wait until their volume increases before concluding, "Oh, now we need a second one." If they had done a little bit of planning with a superstar consultant, they would have known that they could have flipped the layout around and had a shared control room for the two CTs, which would have been much more efficient. But now, because they didn't plan ahead, they need two separate control rooms, which means they probably need twice the number of people running the machines, at a total cost of $100,000 per person. Advice from a superstar on issues like this can make a tremendous difference.

▶ *Poor marketing and education.* If the hospital doesn't educate physicians on how and when to use this technology, the patients will not be well served and the hospital will not reap the full rewards from its investment. If the operators of the equipment are insufficiently trained, patients could even be harmed.

▶ *Getting fired.* If any of these things go wrong, the hospital is going to point to Dr. Murphy and say, "The system won't work without adequate air conditioning. You were responsible for that." What's she going to say: "I didn't think I had to worry about that"? If she doesn't manage the project well, her job may be on the line. This purchase is high stakes for everyone concerned.

▶ *Poor service and support.* The vendor told Dr. Murphy that she would receive great support, but in fact she does not. Why was she blindsided by that? Why does she have that headache? Her response might be, "Well, the sales rep *said* we'd have great service." Dr. Murphy listened to the rep and relied only upon that.

Let's expand on this last point a bit. Just asking sales reps if their company provides good postinstallation service is not the best way to go about the acquisition of a

SECRET WEAPON 1

Request for Vendor References

CORPORATION

Dear [Vendor]:

To help us evaluate your equipment and service, please supply contact information for five of your customers, those closest to our hospital, who have purchased a system similar to the one we're considering buying. Thank you.

Sincerely,

Alice

Alice Murphy, MD
Medical Director of Radiology

Hospital	Contact Person	Phone	Equipment Installed	Installation Date

multimillion-dollar piece of technology. Dr. Murphy shouldn't listen to the rep. Nor should she bring in the vendor's service manager, who will just sing the same "We Provide Good Service" tune. If she is planning on purchasing a CT, or making any major investment for that matter, she is probably considering three vendors. You should advise her to investigate the service records of all three vendors by talking to other nearby customers who have purchased similar products.

Your job as a superstar sales rep is to lead her through that process. Your job is to help her gather unbiased information about all the vendors – including potentially negative information about your company and potentially positive information about the competition – *as if you had no stake in the outcome*. I'll explain why in a moment, after we discuss how to go about it.

You draft a letter (**Secret Weapon 1**) for Dr. Murphy to send to all three vendors. After Dr. Murphy collects that information from each of the three vendors (including you), you help her draft a Vendor Report Card (**Secret Weapon 2**).

Dr. Murphy's team makes several phone calls and asks other hospital administrators to give the vendor a grade of A through F on each item. Now she's ascertained the real story, not just what the sales reps say. Only a superstar consultant can help a customer put that process together.

Perhaps you think this strategy foolishly puts your own company on the line. What if the news about your company's service record isn't good? First of all, now that you are aware of an issue, you can fix it. Second, all is not lost because you have a service issue. That is a large benefit of working with the customer to develop the questions she will ask. Perhaps part of your system has some reliability issues, but your *service response* to these issues has been great. In that case, be sure to include a question that addresses the quality of the service response.

As you evaluate the scores on the Vendor Report Cards, don't be dismayed if you do not come out on top. At the end of the day, do people buy rationally or emotionally? As we'll see in chapter 2, they buy emotionally. Dr. Murphy is going to trust you more for leading her through the process. She knows no one is perfect. Even if she calls your other customers and hears negative reports about your company or product, if she trusts you she will rationalize the comment and think, "Well, only one of the customers told us the truth." That's the whole secret of selling: Customers buy for emotional, not rational, reasons. A CT is a CT is a CT. But a sales rep is not a sales rep is not a sales rep – if one of those reps is a superstar.

> ★ **SUPERSTAR SECRET** ★
>
> **The product doesn't matter. Most products or services will do the job. *You* matter.**

SECRET WEAPON 2

Vendor Report Card

Vendor

Survey Respondent

	Grade	Comments
Overall, how good has the service been?		
How well does the equipment run?		
How quickly does the vendor respond?		
Would you recommend this vendor to others?		
How much downtime have you experienced?		

Other comments about this vendor and this equipment:

If you are the sales rep approaching Dr. Murphy about a sale, and you see yourself as someone who is only able to show her the bells and buttons on her new CT scanner, then you're just like every other sales rep. There is no difference, from her perspective, between vendor A, vendor B, and vendor C. But if you step up and say, "Dr. Murphy, I recently helped several other hospitals similar to yours invest in a CT. I believe that I can be of assistance to you in addressing the many challenges associated with this investment." Imagine the relief she will feel. (Do you see what's happened? You've taken off your Vendor cap and replaced it with a hat labeled "Consultant.")

Think of the product or service that you offer. What are all the headaches that you can prevent or cure? Your job is to share all the potential pitfalls in a way that doesn't make the customer feel bad. You might say, "Let me begin to provide assistance to you. Here are some examples of successful installations at other hospitals. Let's begin to lay out a time schedule so that you can get things done on time and look like a superstar in front of your CEO and board. Let's begin the architectural planning of the room in which the CT will be housed. Let's begin to evaluate the air handling, the electrical requirements, the floor loading, the control room for your techs, and so on. After that, there are umpteen different steps that you may not know about, only because you haven't purchased this product before. I'm an expert in this, and I can guide you through all of them."

These umpteen steps are all peripheral to the actual decision of which CT to buy, but they are of paramount importance to the person who is selecting the CT. The buyer of the CT is going to find these things out *somewhere;* he may make a mistake, he may not, he may get frustrated. You want him to find out all these things from *you,* so that you become his trusted advisor.

This is how you can create what I call "stickiness" in customers, developing their inclination to call you with all their project concerns. You show that you are interested in more than just the sale — you're interested in the customer himself and in helping the whole project succeed. In so doing, you gain a tremendous amount of trust. I have seen many sales reps fail to understand this. In fact, some actually complain when a customer calls for assistance on a non-product-specific issue. They just don't get it. The fact is, you want the customer to rely on you for non-product issues also. This way you are cementing yourself as a trusted advisor and consultant. And when it comes down to determining which product the customer wants to go with, you become his logical solution, because you've been his trusted advisor all along. That's one of the secrets of the superstar: to go way beyond your product or service so that customers recognize you as a true consultant in your field.

A customer might dig in her heels if she does not believe that you are unbiased. You must impress upon her your commitment to acting in her best interest. The superstar learns quickly that the product itself is not all that important. Instead, the superstar goes beyond the product to ask, "How I can provide genuine assistance to help the customer improve the bottom line, get rid of the fifty-patient backlog in the CT service department, increase the hospital's revenue, and reduce the hospital's costs?" If you can't genuinely help the customer with your solution, then you need to think about a new job, with a new product — because you are *not* going to be very successful.

> **★ SUPERSTAR SECRET ★**
>
> **Go above and beyond. Provide assistance way beyond your product or service so that customers recognize you as a true consultant in your field.**

In my workshops for GE salespeople, I ask, "When selling a complex, technical product or service to your customer, who is in the best position to assist the customer with all the necessary steps to plan for, procure, prepare the site, install, train, and support the product under consideration? Let's make it even more clear. How many CTs has your customer purchased in the last three years? Maybe one. How many CTs have you and your support team helped customers invest in over the past three years? Hundreds! Who's in the best position to assist customers and prevent their headaches? The answer points to you-you-you in the audience. You're the reps! You're the ones who know this – you're the ones who can be of help."

In high-tech, big-ticket sales such as software or a CT scanner, the consulting extends to a very important early step, which is developing the business case for the product – that is, what the business might expect to spend – and gain – from its purchase. This has to be done early on. If I, as Dr. Murphy, were to hire an outside consultant to help me buy a CT, one of the services I would expect from that consultant is the business case. So why shouldn't you as the CT sales rep be doing that?

Many companies offering big-ticket services, software, or high-tech products provide some type of financial analysis to share with customers. Prepared in an unbiased fashion and used effectively, the business case helps you earn trust and position yourself as a true consultant.

Blocking Outside Consultants

My goal is to get rid of the outside consultants in the world – the third parties who are hired to "help" a customer with a major purchase and get between my customers and me. My customers shouldn't need outside consultants to advise them on what I'm selling. If I'm working with a customer and the customer hires an outside consultant, this is an indication that I'm not doing my job.

Outside consultants serve as intermediaries between the sales rep and the customer. They undermine the sales process, triangulating what should be a one-on-one relationship. Once inside your customer's organization, outside consultants eat information, and they use the information they take from you to negotiate against you. Outside consultants ruin the sales rep's ability to gain trust in the customer's mind, because the outside consultants are out there waving the flag, trying to capture all the value and gain all the customer accolades. The sales rep is relegated to the role of a gofer providing pricing – the technician selling the widget, no longer the trusted advisor.

You do not want to be there. The key to keeping outside consultants out is to do your job and do it well. Your goal is to serve as the customer's inside consultant. Then there will be no need for the customer to look elsewhere for sound advice.

Solver or Avoider?

In a study done by a marketing and sales magazine some years ago, only about 5% of salespeople qualified as true consultative sales reps. The remaining 95% were product peddlers (55%), also known as technical folks or engineering geeks, and visitors (40%), also known as Doughnut Dollies or Doughnut Dans, reps who stop in now and then with goodies. Of the consultative reps, some were problem solvers and some were problem avoiders. Both problem solvers and problem avoiders are superstars, but one is a bit better than the other.

Problem solvers must be informed of a problem by the customer before they take action. After that, they help the customer solve the problem. This is valuable assistance, but I encourage you to do even more for the customer. Problem avoiders are so involved in the customer's business that they anticipate potential problems before the customer is aware of any issues. Do not wait for problems to show up in your customer's business; your job is to prevent the problems before they happen. In the case of an approaching tsunami, a problem solver would be first on the scene, delivering valuable assistance to those affected by the giant wave. The problem avoider, on the other hand, sees the tsunami coming, warns everyone in its path, and gets everyone to safety, therefore saving lives.

▶ The Superstar Test ◀

What is a superstar? How will you know when you get there? There are three ways to tell:

Superstar Indicator 1: Customers Follow You

If you leave your company, do your customers follow you to your new company? If you leave the industry, do the customers have such a strong desire to continue to work with you that they'll pay high fees for you to consult on their next purchase? This shows that you're providing incremental value above and beyond – as opposed to simply representing your product. Anyone can represent a product, but not everyone can consult with his or her customers and act as an unpaid advisor.

The greatest reward of superstar selling is the long-term relationships with customers who remember long after the fact the value you brought to them. I am frequently surprised and pleased when I meet new GE people and they say, "Oh, *you're* the Dan Adams that my customers continue to ask me about!" Customers remember me not because I took them golfing or dropped by with doughnuts but because I consistently brought them value.

Superstar Indicator 2: Telling the Truth

A superstar shows a willingness to simply and honestly state the facts. Sounds simple, doesn't it? Most sales reps seem to forget this basic rule. It comes into play when you do not have the correct solution to meet the long-term needs of the customer. At GE I would occasionally receive a request for a particular GE product, one that was not well suited for a particular type of orthopedic procedure because it was underpowered. Rather than risk my long-term relationship with the customer, I would provide the names and phone numbers of my competitors – those who had a more suitable solution – and strongly suggest that the customer contact them. You have to be willing to say to the customer, "My solution may work in the short term, but it really is not a good long-term fit for you. Here is the contact info for a competitor of mine who has a product that I believe will much better suit your long-term needs."

Caution! When you see how well customers respond to your consultative style and to your willingness to put their needs before your own, you may feel like telling all your customers to buy from the competition. *Wrong.* This approach should be used only in rare instances. If you find yourself using this Disengage strategy (see page 116) too often, then you are working for a company that is not in touch with its customers' needs – and you're working for the wrong company.

A slight slant on this idea is when a customer wants to buy from you but you believe that buying nothing at all is in the best interests of the customer. A magnetic resonance (MR) customer once called me up and said, "Dan, guess what? We are so busy with the two MR scanners that we bought from you that we are now ready to buy a third MR." I said, "That's great, Dr. Gannon. And I would love to sell it to you. But what if I provide an evaluation of how you are utilizing your two current systems to see if we can suggest some ideas to help you to avoid or delay the need for that third system?" The hospital allowed us to analyze its level of efficiency and we later received the order for the third MR and millions of dollars in incremental business. My relationship with that customer was locked in forever.

Superstar Indicator 3: No Excuses

"Why did we lose that deal?" is a routine question that managers ask their reps. One simple way to identify the superstars in the crowd is to analyze the responses. Most reps will reply, "We didn't get the support we needed from headquarters," or "We don't have feature A or B," or "Our price was too high, wah wah wah." If that were the case, why is it that every single day, sales reps are winning deals in which their price is significantly higher than everyone else's?

The response from a superstar will be short and sweet: "I was outsold" or "I didn't earn their trust." A superstar knows that customers do not buy based on the product or service; they buy based on their level of trust in the sales rep. A superstar does not make excuses. It's not just that she is good at fessing up – it's more than that. Superstars understand how people make decisions. Bad reps think people make decisions based on price or features. Superstar reps know people make decisions based on whether or not they trust and rely on you (see the Trust Triangle, page 34). So if a superstar loses a sale, she says, "I was outsold. I didn't qualify the opportunity correctly, I didn't get to the decision maker, I didn't uncover their needs adequately, or I didn't understand the customer's buying or decision-making process. This all about me-me-me." The average loser rep says, "It's all about something else."

Take a moment to look in a mirror. If you were to evaluate your performance as a sales rep so far, to what extent are those three superstar indicators already present? Do your customers follow you? Do you tell customers the truth? And do you refuse to make excuses? If you're not there yet, don't worry. This book is all about telling you how to get there.

▶ Do You Have What It Takes to Be a Superstar? ◀

The short answer is probably yes. You've gone through a screening process; you're working for a company; you have probably already made some sales. Superstar reps have certain innate qualities in differing degrees. I call them the ABCDE qualities: ambition, brains, conscience, drive, and empathy. If you've chosen a career in sales, by definition you probably possess them.

Ambition

Ambition means wanting to be the best, wanting to constantly improve. It doesn't mean being overbearing or stepping on people on your way to the top. A superstar has the ability to project himself into the future and imagine great things – then take the necessary steps to get there.

One of the things that drives superstars is competition. GE started publishing a leader board, known vernacularly as the "rack and stack." The leader board ranked rep performance by sales. The top 10% were then rewarded with free trips and membership in GE's equivalent of a President's Club. Prior to the publishing of the leader board, I was frustrated as a salesperson by the lack of feedback. I knew how *I* was doing with my accounts, but, except for the gossip around the water cooler, I had no idea how I compared with other reps across the country. Therefore, I had no way of measuring my success. For superstars, such feedback is essential, because learning that you're not doing well forces you to work that much harder.

Brains

A superstar has to think strategically. It's not enough to be a nice person with a warm smile and a lot of product knowledge. You need the brainpower to constantly assess the flow of the customer conversation, absorb complex processes, and integrate them brilliantly. Superstars, while focusing on the details with the customer, also see the whole process from thirty thousand feet. Although they are empathic and friendly, their actions are ruled by their thinking, not by their emotions. They have the wisdom to walk away from deals that are not win-win (see page 24). Superstars carefully observe the consequences of their choices and learn from their mistakes. They possess keen judgment.

Conscience

A superstar cares about duty to others. He has the integrity and the courage to do the right thing and tell the truth, even when the truth is unpleasant. Conscience is somewhat related to class — not class in the sense of wealth or social status but in the way one treats others. It has nothing to do with status symbols and everything to do with standards of behavior. It all boils down to how you conduct yourself with customers and colleagues. Do you choose to be a pro… or a schmo?

Qualities of a Superstar

Ambition
A passion for success. Thinking big. Hungering for more out of life.

Brains
The strategic thinking necessary to assess the flow of the customer conversation, absorb complex processes, and integrate them brilliantly.

Conscience
Integrity that demands that you follow high principles and behave reliably and honestly.

Drive
The competitive spirit that pushes you to win. The determination and tenacity to stick with a task until it is done.

Empathy
The ability to imagine yourself in someone else's shoes. Warmth and genuine concern that engender customers' trust and respect.

Drive

Drive is the desire to win, the push to succeed (but it doesn't mean being overbearing). It would be very tough to be successful in sales without drive. Because it's such a hard field, you have to continue to push. Sometimes fear can supply the necessary competitive drive. Other times it is the challenge of the hunt or the promise of high compensation.

Superstars have courage and tenacity – they feel fear, just like everyone else, but they don't let it stop them. They have strong backbones, which doesn't mean they are rigid or inflexible – it means they have the steadfastness and fortitude to regain their enthusiasm for the job even after major disappointments.

The superstar sales rep learns from each failure and uses those lessons to become stronger. She continues to get back up after being pushed down time and time again – she's like a kid's clown punching bag, self-righting herself after every hit. If you find it difficult to get back up again, you may be in the wrong field. You're not going to be successful – at least in the high-stakes sales world in which I played. However, you may be successful in other areas of sales that aren't as highly competitive.

Empathy

Empathy is the ability to see yourself in another's shoes. You've heard of ventriloquists who can throw their voices? Empathy is like throwing your mind and heart into the body of another.

I was told when I was hired at GE that I was the only sales rep with just an MBA. All my colleagues and all my competitors were engineers – technical widget guys. The thought in some people's minds was that a guy like me couldn't succeed, because I couldn't understand the electronics, the high technology, or the physics involved in making magnetic resonance imaging (MRI) machines. I proved them all wrong, for two reasons. First, because the technical stuff was hard for me, I quickly learned that when a customer asks, "What time is it?" she does not want to know how to build a watch. She simply wants to know the time. Second, thanks to my business degree, I was mindful of the critical considerations involved in making sound business decisions. I had empathy for what customers were going through when facing significant investments. If you put yourself in the customers' shoes, you begin to have a sense of the pain they're experiencing. If you can latch onto that pain, it has a huge impact on every interaction with the customer.

What kind of pain do customers feel? Imagine yourself as Samuel Watt, the CFO of a large food company who's been given the responsibility of selecting his company's new procurement software. Mr. Watt neither sought out this responsibility nor does he feel up to the task of fulfilling it. He has rarely purchased this type of large software solution before — or anything like it. He has just talked with three reps. Every one of them came in and described the technical facts and features of their product and how much better their product is than the competitors'. His head is spinning. He doesn't want to deal with reps like that. He's thinking, "What a hassle! None of these reps is helping *me*."

If you, thinking like a *consultative* sales rep, put yourself in Mr. Watt's shoes and realize that this person has to report to the CEO on the success of the project, then you start thinking about what services you can provide to make him successful. You ask yourself, "What does Mr. Watt need right now? What will he need tomorrow?" And you start putting together a plan to help him.

> ★ SUPERSTAR SECRET ★
>
> **Imagine for a moment that the customer is your mother. Doesn't that immediately shift your attitude into ultra-empathy mode?**

Your empathy should also extend to yourself and your colleagues. To be a superstar, you need self-awareness and personal insight, a willingness to accept feedback on the gap between how you think you're coming across to others and how you're actually coming across. It's important to see how what you're saying is landing on the other side of the table and to understand how subtle differences in words and shifts in body language can make all the difference in communicating what you mean. Empathy requires that you are fully aware of — and willing to own up to — your true attitudes and feelings.

If you find it difficult for whatever reason to empathize with a customer — perhaps she's cranky, or doesn't look like you, or has irritating habits — try this exercise: Imagine for a moment that the customer is your mother. Doesn't that immediately shift your attitude into ultra-empathy mode? Aren't you instantly on the customer's side, wanting to help, instead of wanting to argue or fight? If imagining the customer as your mother doesn't work, try imagining her as your best friend, or as the person you admire most in the world. *That's* what your relationship with your customers should be like: ethical, honest, and helpful, willing to serve the customer's best interests.

► All Superstars Are Not Alike ◄

As we said earlier, all superstar sales reps have these five traits: ambition, brains, conscience, drive, and empathy. It's a mathematical formula: $A + B + C + D + E =$ Superstar. The quantities of each subjective element in the formula are not fixed, however; we each have a different mix — our own Personal Sales Formula. You might have low C and E, but high A, B, and D. Your drive, or D, might be higher than that of the person next to you, while your empathy, or E, might be slightly lower.

It's the combination of those qualities that bring success. You can't have drive – and no empathy. And you can't be all empathy and no drive (if you were, you'd have a different occupation; you wouldn't be a sales rep).

A colleague's twenty-year-old son is a perfect example of a Personal Sales Formula that may bring success. He is very much a people person. He has tons of friends, his phone is always ringing, and his friends know that they can count on him in a pinch. He is about to take a job in sales. He wants to excel, especially in the eyes of his peers. He seems, however, to have very low drive. He is not used to taking the initiative or accepting responsibility for his screw-ups. He may turn out to be very successful, though, because despite his low drive, the other parts of his Personal Sales Formula – conscience, ambition, and brains – are quite high. He also happens to empathize easily, which reminds us of the one quality essential to all superstars: E – empathy. It's so important that we'll revisit it in chapter 2.

Take a moment to reflect on your own Personal Sales Formula. If you were to draw a graph showing the degree to which you possess each of the five superstar qualities (ambition, brains, conscience, drive, and empathy), which bar would be tallest? Shortest?

In addition to these inherent personal qualities, a superstar has certain skills, such as controlling the customer's buying process, employing the right strategy, and negotiating effectively – all of which can be learned. We'll discuss these in future chapters.

Personal Sales Formula

A sales rep needs all these characteristics to become a superstar. A strength in one area may compensate for a relative weakness in another.

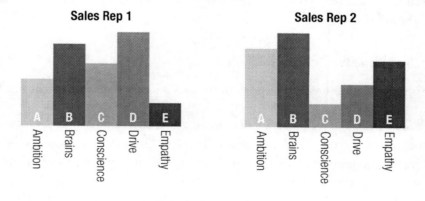

Sales Rep 1

A – Ambition   B – Brains   C – Conscience   D – Drive   E – Empathy

Sales Rep 2

A – Ambition   B – Brains   C – Conscience   D – Drive   E – Empathy

▶ What You Don't Need ◀

Extroversion

Oddly enough, what you don't need to become a superstar sales pro is to be a people person, or an extrovert — an engaging type who goes to a party and connects with everyone instantly, who has thousands of friends, who loves to tell stories, and who is often the center of attention. Everyone likes to talk with such extroverted folks. They are charismatic and interact well with others.

An extrovert gets energy and feels alive when surrounded by lots of people, with a high degree of interaction. In contrast, an introvert's idea of a really good time is an evening by herself with a book. Extroverts tend to migrate toward sales — as opposed to desk jobs or accounting. Oftentimes they do well. But I would submit that they do well as long as their Personal Sales Formula has other strengths — because to become a sales superstar, more is required than just glad-handing.

> **★ SUPERSTAR SECRET ★**
>
> **Buyers who might not choose you for a friend will buy from you if they trust and respect you.**

In the old world of sales, extroverts were assumed to be headed toward careers as sales reps. The uncle who had a joke for every occasion, Miss Congeniality in high school…. People would say to them, "You ought to go into sales!" Sales reps were recruited based on their extroversion. They were given a test, which asked, "Would you rather read a book, go to a party, or see a movie?" If the candidate picked "read a book," the testers would conclude the candidate would be no good at sales. Wrong.

I don't have high people skills. I would feel uncomfortable going to a party, meeting a lot of people, and making a bunch of new friends. That would not be fun for me. The ability to connect with people — to have empathy for them, to imagine yourself in their shoes — is indeed necessary. But joke telling and being the life of the party are not.

Excessive Likability

Surprisingly, likability is less important to sales success than one might think.

> **Situation A.** You walk into a diner and sit down on a stool. Mildred, the waitress behind the counter, is charming and friendly. She's exactly the sort of person you'd gravitate to at a party. She's attractive and appealing — but she gets everything wrong. You order coffee black; it comes with a stack of creamers on the saucer. You order a tuna fish sandwich on rye; you get whole wheat instead. You *like* Mildred, but you don't respect her abilities as a waitress, nor do you trust her to take care of your needs. Will you come back to this diner?

Situation B. You need to have brain surgery. You meet with a surgeon whose personality and mannerisms you don't particularly like – he's gruff, he interrupts you a lot, and you don't like the way he dresses. But from what you've heard, he is the best in the country at what he does. You respect his abilities and trust that he'll do a good job. Do you care how likable he is?

Jacques Werth, president of High Probability® Selling, analyzed the results of several studies exploring the factors most important to someone making a significant purchase. The bold numbers (below) indicate what percentage of respondents listed this factor in their top five buying decision factors. Trust in the sales rep was the most important factor (87%). Respect for the sales rep was a close second (82%). Only after trust and respect did the reputation of the company or product (76%) and product features (71%) emerge as factors. After that, the buyers considered quality and service (58%) and then price (16%). One of the least important factors – twelfth on the list, in fact – was the likability of the sales rep (3%).

I'm not suggesting that you go out of your way to be unlikable. Don't get surly to get ahead. I'm pointing out that buyers who might not choose you for a friend will buy from you if they trust and respect you. If they do not trust and respect you, the chances that they will buy are low. But if the customers respect you, quite logically they may end up being your friend – but not necessarily. A equals B, but B does not necessarily equal C. So just because they like you doesn't mean they're going to buy. If they trust you, they'll buy – and oftentimes that leads to their liking you as well.

Buying Decision Factors

1 Level of trust in the salesperson: **87%**

2 Level of respect for the salesperson: **82%**

3 Reputation of the company or product: **76%**

4 Features of the product or service: **71%**

5 Quality and service: **58%**

6 Price (non-commodity): **16%**

12 Like the salesperson (rapport): **3%**

Source: Jacques Werth. "The Ultimate Competitive Advantage: Trust and Respect."

► Only Win-Win Deals ◄

In traditional selling there are four possible kinds of deals: *win-win,* in which both you and the customer are satisfied with the deal and the business relationship; *win-lose,* in which you feel good about the sale but the customer doesn't; *lose-win,* in which you feel you had to buy the business, but the customer is happy; and *lose-lose,* in which everyone walks away unhappy, and you're unlikely to do business together again.

No sales rep in her right mind wants to be anywhere but win-win all the time. A true superstar believes that it is impossible for the rep to win and the customer to lose. A superstar is interested in the long term and cannot envision a situation, over the long run, in which the rep would benefit if the customer lost. In other words, although a rep may win a battle, if the customer believes that he lost the battle you can bet that in the long run the rep will lose the war. Superstars, always looking at the big picture, never have a sense of a win if the customer lost.

> ★ **SUPERSTAR SECRET** ★
>
> **You fall down so you can learn how to get up.**

If I ever faced a win-lose situation — in which I could win, but at my customer's expense (for instance, by talking him into something he didn't need, or selling him a solution that truly didn't benefit him) — I would walk away from the deal. This isn't just good ethics; it's good business sense. I am interested in long-term relationships, and if I win a sale in which the customer loses, I will never get any more deals from that customer. In the sales world in which I played, long-term success was crucial.

Once I benefited from another rep's short-term, win-lose approach. A lowly rep from a competing firm went after an immediate sale by plugging a square peg into a round hole. Through price discounting, the rep persuaded a major hospital to purchase a piece of equipment that turned out to be poorly designed and dismally ineffective for this customer. The rep knew the equipment was not going to meet the customer's needs, but still pushed for the sale. When the customer found this out, he was furious. For the next twenty-plus years, that hospital refused to deal with that rep's company. Instead, it often chose to do business with me.

There are rare instances in which lose-win (buying the business) is appropriate — but only on a short-term basis in order to achieve a long-term win. I will occasionally do such a deal because I know there will be benefits down the road, such as a reference, getting traction in the target company, and so on.

► How to Lose a Sale and Win ◄

I hate losing. Losing is hard. If you're a sales pro, you know that people buy or don't buy because of *you*. You can't help but take it personally. Losing is particularly tough in the world of high-ticket sales, where we're talking not about a turkey sandwich or a hundred-dollar pair of shoes but multimillion-dollar sales that require a great deal of effort — sometimes a year or more of losing sleep and working long hours.

Consultative selling doesn't make losing any easier. Once you understand what a customer needs and you have a solution that fits those needs, you feel strongly that your solution is the correct solution. So if the customer selects someone else, it just adds to the pain. You know that you didn't do your job, you worry that the customer doesn't trust you, you think you're not successful. You conclude that you're no good, you're not a winner — in fact, you're a loser!

For me, luckily — unlike salespeople in some situations — losing a sale never meant not putting food on the table; we were a double-income family. I hate losing because I'm extremely competitive. I simply do not want to lose!

Consultative selling reframes some of these so-called losses. Even though you don't win the sale, you maintain the long-term relationship with the customer — and that is a win (see Secret Weapon 34 — Loss Letter, page 153). You maintain your credibility and your own integrity — that's another win. Gather up what you've learned and declare that as your prize.

Sometimes you'll win by actively choosing to lose — by recommending that the customer seek out a competitor's solution. This is the right thing to do if what you have to offer is not in the customer's best interests. Again, the wins in this case are maintaining your credibility and a long-term customer relationship.

> ★ **SUPERSTAR SECRET** ★
>
> **Never lose twice for the same reason.**

In the 2005 movie *Batman Begins,* Batman asks his father, "Why do we fall?" The father replies, "So we can learn how to get up." Superstars fall down, too — but never twice for the same reason. They learn from their mistakes. That's how you really win by losing. You send a loss letter, which is another way to win by losing. And you don't go whining and crying — that is *not* a superstar.

In the next chapter we'll take a close look at the world of sales as viewed through the customer's eyes and provide techniques that will make you more effective — so you *don't* lose.

CHAPTER TWO

HOW CUSTOMERS MAKE DECISIONS

Learning to sell like a superstar involves mastering three processes:

- ► First, you come to understand the Customer Decision Process and learn how to climb the Trust Triangle (discussed here).
- ► Second, you develop, document, and drive (D^3) the Customer Buying Process (chapter 3).
- ► Third, you master the steps of the Superstar Selling Process (chapter 4).

Trust Triangle Selling

Buyer
Decision Process   Buying Process

Seller
Superstar Selling Process

The bulk of the literature on selling and on sales force education focuses on the last step, the sales process. The irony is that it is the least important of the three processes. Therefore, we will discuss the sales process last (in chapter 4) instead of first.

► Empathy, the Secret Ingredient ◄

Empathy is the key to understanding how customers make decisions. As we mentioned earlier, empathy is the ability to throw one's heart and mind into the body of another person — and see how it feels to be that person. It's a skill essential to becoming a superstar. Thankfully, it's one that can be developed.

The next time you have a free hour or two, visit various retail establishments in your community with this goal: to see how it feels to get "sold." Visit two types of establishments: ones in which you're more likely to encounter old-school sales reps and ones in which you're more likely to encounter consultative (even superstar) reps.

The first category usually includes places such as used-car salesrooms and discount clothing stores. The second category usually includes high-end clothing stores (such as Mark Shale), custom audio firms (such as Audio Consultants in Hinsdale, Illinois), and luxury car dealerships (such as Mercedes Benz or BMW). There are exceptions, of course; you might run into a superstar sales rep at a TJ Maxx and an old-school rep at a BMW dealer. You never know.

★ SUPERSTAR SECRET ★

As a starting point, treat customers the way you would like to be treated. Then follow my Modified Golden Rule: Treat customers the way _they_ would like to be treated.

Try to visit at least six establishments — three in each category. Visit the hard-sell places first, then the softer-sell places. Pretend you're a serious customer. Get sold. Go all the way through the sales process up to the point of handing over your credit card. Don't follow any particular script — just be yourself, buying a car. Be sure to respect the sales rep's time. Don't take time away from their other customers if the showroom is packed.

During your visit, pay attention to the following:

► How does it feel to walk in the door? What is the ambience?

► What do you like and not like about the environment?

► How does the sales rep treat you (and your companion, if someone accompanies you)?

► Are your emotional needs being met — that is, do you feel valued as a customer, listened to, and respected?

- ► Are your needs for factual information getting met?

- ► Do you trust the rep? If yes, at what point in the interaction does the trust kick in? What does she do or say that engenders your trust?

- ► Does the rep seem to trust you? (For example, at the car dealership, does the rep ask you for your driver's license before he allows you to test drive the car with him?)

- ► Do you respect the rep? At what point do you begin to respect him? From the moment the rep walks up to you? Or afterward?

- ► Does the sales rep respond to your own needs or push her own agenda?

Jot down some notes right after you leave each establishment. Pay attention to what you are thinking and how you are feeling — and what triggered those reactions. How did it feel to go from the hard sell of the used-car dealership to the highly consultative soft sell of the BMW showroom?

People who do this exercise usually come back with observations such as these:

- ► "I didn't like the way the sales rep treated me."
- ► "The sales rep seemed to care about me."
- ► "The sales rep talked with my husband, but not with me."
- ► "The sales rep pushed features that were irrelevant to me."
- ► "The sales rep was dressed for the part."
- ► "The sales rep tried to push me into signing a contract before I was ready."
- ► "The sales rep interrupted me, and I didn't like that."
- ► "The sales rep asked me what I wanted, and I liked that a lot."
- ► "The sales rep rushed me."
- ► "The sales rep remembered my name, and I was pleasantly surprised."
- ► "The sales rep made insulting assumptions about what I wanted to buy."
- ► "The sales rep greeted me warmly, as if genuinely happy to see me."

Pay attention to your reactions so you can mold the behaviors you like into your own selling style — and edit out the behaviors you don't like. If you don't like it when a sales rep interrupts you, then don't do that when you're selling. This emulation of selling behaviors is logical, but all too often sales reps forget this. Out of habit, they continue to treat their customers in ways that they themselves do not like to be treated. As a starting point, treat customers the way you would like to be treated. Then follow my Modified Golden Rule: Treat customers the way *they* would like to be treated.

Get out there. Pay attention. Put yourself in your customers' shoes, imagining how they would feel if you treated them the same way. Every customer interaction brings with it opportunities for you to shine where other reps might not. I call these moments superstar turning points, or STPs. Don't miss them. Watch for chances to be a true consultant instead of an old-school rep.

► The Product Doesn't Matter ◄

True or false: A sales rep's success is tied directly to the quality of the product or solution she is offering. As a buyer visiting car dealerships, you may have thought you were comparing car A with car B. But actually, what you were really comparing was sales rep A with sales rep B. That's what happens in customers' minds. The sales rep acts as the intermediary between the customer and the product or service, greatly influencing how people buy. The customer bases his decision, for the most part, on the actions of this intermediary (that is, *if* the sales rep is a superstar). After all, a car is a car is a car. Any of them will get you where you want to go. Yes, the sales rep does have to have a decent product. But in most cases the solutions are very similar, and it's the rep who makes the difference. The rep enjoys a position between the product and the customer's perception of that product. It is the sales rep who can make that product look worse than, equal to, or better than the competitor's product. Superstars know that the difference between the products is really the difference that the superstar brings to the table in the form of consultative selling skills. Superstars differentiate themselves not by *what* they sell but by *how* they sell.

> ★ SUPERSTAR SECRET ★
>
> **Superstars differentiate themselves not by *what* they sell but by *how* they sell.**

If the sales rep is *not* a superstar, then the customer makes the decision based on price and features. With no superstar rep in the picture, the customer's decision is easy: Buy the one with the lowest price.

One thing that drew me to sales training was realizing the difference a great rep can make to a company. We've all had a chance to observe this. Consider what happens to a company when one of its superstars leaves a territory — sales drop almost immediately. The converse is true when an experienced consultant is placed in a new territory — sales immediately increase. What changed? Has the company drastically reduced price, changed its marketing strategy, or announced a new product? No. After more than twenty years of witnessing this, I have seen time and time again that the cause of the sales drop is the departure of that particular superstar. This proves that the sales rep is critical!

► How People Buy ◄

People buy because they want to avoid pain or solve a problem. They want to experience the positive benefits of your solution. They want to achieve some value greater than the cost. Their decisions are made emotionally and then justified rationally.

Most of us have purchased homes. When you buy a home, you usually make a decision based on your very first impression as you turn into the driveway – an emotional decision. Next, you enter the home and visualize yourself in it. You can see your couch here, your recliner there, and wouldn't your TV be perfect over there? These are all emotional decisions. Then what happens? You make an offer contingent upon the home inspection and financing. The inspection tells you whether the house is structurally sound or has problems. The appraiser tells you whether you are in the ballpark with regard to price. You've made an emotional decision and justified it rationally.

When people buy cars, they demonstrate the point perfectly. If I asked you about your car's braking distance, horsepower, torque, and 0-to-60 elapsed time, could you provide the data? Buying a car meets an emotional need, whether it is security or a desire for status or a sporty image. Most people buy what they consider to be a cool car – and justify it later.

I recently walked into a showroom to buy a car. The sales rep immediately opened the hood and inundated me with facts about the engine's might. This, of course, is exactly what he *should not* have done. What could he have done instead? He could have asked me a series of high-value questions to get me thinking about my car ownership experience. He could have started out by asking what I like and don't like about my current car. If I had raised reliability as a concern, he could have said, "Before we look at that car, let's go back into my service department. I would like to show you how you will be treated *after* you buy a car from me. Look at my engineers – they are impeccably dressed. They are the best educated, most highly trained automotive service technicians in the state. You could almost eat off the service department floor. If anything at all happens to your car, we will personally take it from your garage to ours, and we will fix it good as new. We're going to take care of you *after* the sale. Why should you care about this? Because you can get this exact same car from ten dealerships in this state. How we take care of you after the sale is what clearly distinguishes us."

> ★ SUPERSTAR SECRET ★
>
> **Buyer decisions are made emotionally and then justified rationally.**

This is much better than what you hear traditionally from a car salesperson, isn't it?

What kind of watch do you wear on your wrist? Before you bought it, did you research its degree of precision and read up on the inner workings of watches? Did you study *Consumer Reports?* Or did you model it on your wrist to see how good it looked? Did you buy it for the status? Buying an expensive watch that looks good on your wrist is an emotional decision. This is how most of us buy a watch.

I buy for the same reasons. Not long ago my wife and I went shopping at Crate and Barrel, where she urged me to look at some colorful hand-painted dishes. She loved them, and they were perfect with our décor. After selecting coordinating napkins, glasses, and accessories, we hauled the pile of dishes to the checkout counter. The clerk congratulated us on our exquisite taste in dinnerware, but added, "You might want to know that these cannot go into the dishwasher. You have to wash them by hand, or the glaze will be ruined." Even in the face of such a compelling and rational reason not to buy, what do you think we did? And guess who is doing the dishes?

When I was working for GE, I would routinely get a call from a key decision maker just before a deal was set to close. It would be a doctor or a senior executive from the hospital calling just a day prior to finalizing a multimillion-dollar deal. Why do you think he was calling? He would say yes, he would be recommending my solution tomorrow, but could I please send him a one-page justification for *his* decision? Typically, I had been working closely with this customer for a year or more, hammering out every detail of the project. He fully trusted that I would take care of his needs, but he needed a reminder of the *rational justification* for his *emotional decision.*

If it's true that customers make vendor selections based on an emotional perception of the superiority of one vendor's offering versus others, and if most offerings are indeed similar, then how does a superstar win? Well, you could try to become a product expert, offering to build a watch for the customer each time she asks you for the time. This will not work in most selling situations. In order to differentiate your product you must first differentiate yourself. Once you have differentiated yourself, the customer will make it easier for you to differentiate your offering. Even though your offering is similar to those from other vendors, the customer perceives and justifies a significant difference because of you! What's the best way for you to differentiate yourself? Serve as a true consultant to your customer, guiding her through all the headaches of a major purchase.

The next time you approach one of your customers, remind yourself of the many decisions you have made emotionally that you justify rationally later. Have some understanding of what your buyer is going through, and what is important to him emotionally. I'm more empathetic with my customers when I consider how I would represent my mother in a buying situation. Think about how you would react, for instance, if your mother called you and said, "Honey, I've decided to buy a computer so I can send e-mail and use the Internet. Will you help me pick one out?" I think you would act as a true consultant for your mother's benefit. Your first response would be to ask some questions about how she plans to use her new computer. By doing this you increase her trust in your ability to advise her. The ability to gain trust is the superstar's most critical trait.

▸ Informal versus Formal Decision Making ◂

In every large, complex sale, the customer follows both an emotional (informal) and rational (formal) decision-making process. When you bought your house, after you found a number of homes that felt right (the emotional component of the decision), you probably compared square footage, number of bedrooms, and asking prices (the rational component). Buyers of big-ticket, high-technology products do the same – they rack and stack the various vendors and solutions, sometimes using intricate spreadsheets. A simplified spreadsheet is shown below.

Formal Decision-Making Process

During the formal (or rational) decision-making process, the customer racks and stacks the various vendors and solutions.

Purchase Criterion	Criterion Rank	Vendor A	Vendor B	Vendor C
Initial selling price	1	Excellent ★★★	Poor ★	Poor ★
Service and support	2	Excellent ★★★	Poor ★	Poor ★
Performance	3	Excellent ★★★	Average ★★	Excellent ★★★
Upgradeability	4	Average ★★	Average ★★	Excellent ★★★
Reputation	5	Average ★★	Poor ★	Excellent ★★★

In contrast, the informal decision-making process occurs continually in the mind of the buyer. Both the informal and formal processes are important for the superstar to understand. However, a keen understanding and total command of the informal process is the key to becoming a superstar.

► The Trust Triangle™ ◄

Trust is the key to sales success. Customers will not even listen to you until they trust you. In the film *Meet the Parents* (2000), Jack Byrnes tells Greg Focker, "You're either inside the circle of trust or you're outside. And once you're outside, you can't get back in."

The Trust Triangle is the cornerstone upon which my methodology is based. On the bottom left-hand side of the triangle is a closed-minded customer. The sales rep takes the customer up the left-hand face of the triangle – the emotional side. Once the customer reaches the top of the triangle, he becomes open-minded. The customer's emotional needs have been met and the customer trusts the sales rep. Only then can the sales rep walk the customer down the right face of the triangle – the rational side – toward consummating the sale.

Informal Decision-Making Process

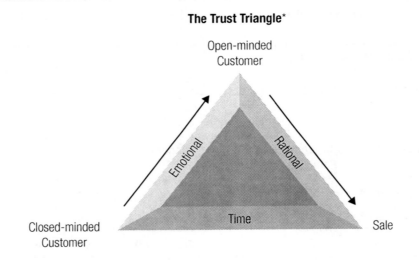

The Trust Triangle*

Open-minded Customer

Emotional   Rational

Time

Closed-minded Customer   Sale

*Adapted from Sam O'Rear.

How do you get the customer to the top of the triangle? In other words, how do you gain the customer's trust? By showing the three Cs: credibility, concern, and just a bit of competence. The consequence of demonstrating these three traits with your customer will be *trust* – confidence on the part of your customer that you have his best interests in mind.

The mistake many sales reps make at this stage of the customer conversation is to overemphasize the competence aspect. By "sufficient competence" I do not mean overwhelming customers with your product knowledge; I mean quietly

Trust Formula

The way to earn a customer's trust is to establish your credibility, show concern for the customer, and display sufficient competence.

$$\frac{\begin{array}{r} \textbf{Credibility} \\ + \quad \textbf{Concern} \\ + \quad \text{Competence} \end{array}}{\textbf{Customer Trust}}$$

and confidently indicating that you are the right person to help them. Should we even have "competence" on the left side of the triangle? Yes, because customers need to be convinced that you are competent to help them. However, your credibility and concern will outshine your competence.

True or false: If a sales rep quickly impresses the customer with her technical prowess, the rep will be successful. Superstars know that customers will never listen to technical details until the rep establishes her credibility. The rep gains credibility by helping the customer with non-solution-specific information that helps the customer to run his business better. It is appropriate to back up the truck and dump technical information on the customer only later in the buying process, and only after the customer is open-minded. Until then, you should never snap open your briefcase, pass out brochures, or conduct a formal presentation because the customer is on the left side of the triangle and is therefore not yet open-minded. Usually the first thing a sales rep wants to show is how competent she is. Fresh from headquarters, she demonstrates her freshly honed product knowledge. The poor customer is the dumpee of countless facts, figures, speeds, feeds, and specs.

Even more important, the sales rep should never unload technical information on the customer before the rep has shown concern for the customer and his needs. Nobody cares how much you know until they know how much you care. So the *last thing* you want to do when you first meet a customer is to talk about your solution.

Once the customer is open-minded, then you can share facts and figures — while continuing to show credibility and concern. The need to show credibility and concern doesn't stop the moment the customer becomes open-minded and trusting.

> ★ **SUPERSTAR SECRET** ★
>
> **The one word that encompasses what it takes to truly become a superstar is *trust*. Trust is confidence that the other person has your best interests in mind.**

Climbing the Trust Triangle

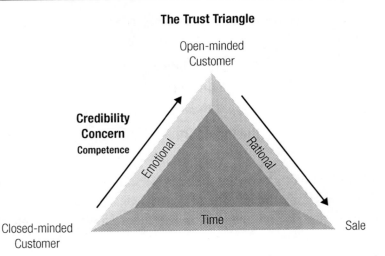

If you begin working with a customer who has already begun the buying process and you are late in the game, you have only one option – to try and delay the decision so that you have time to build trust. For example, let's say you get a call from a customer who announces that he is ready to buy next week. Upon questioning him you discover that the customer is already six months into his buying process.

> ★ SUPERSTAR SECRET ★
>
> **Nobody cares how much you know until they know how much you care.**
> – *Theodore Roosevelt*

You have to resist reacting to the customer's demands. The Trust Triangle reminds us that you must establish trust in the customer's mind before you can expect him to be open-minded to your offering. Your best chance is to delay the decision so that you can work on gaining trust. (See Delay Strategy, page 115.)

How to Gain Credibility and Show Your Concern

To gain trust you must demonstrate credibility and show your concern for the customer. How do you do that? You examine the world from her point of view. Before quotes, presentations, test drives, or demonstrations, *nothing* should be provided to the customer until you fully understand her business, strengths, weaknesses, opportunities, and threats – along with her specific needs, pains, challenges, and concerns. All this information is uncovered in two ways: through research on your own and by asking questions of the customer.

Use web sites to gain information on your customers and their respective industries. Mentioning this research early on will help customers think of you as

Approaching the Sale

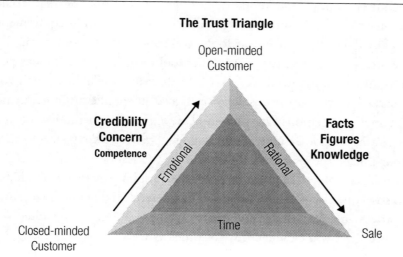

The Trust Triangle

Open-minded
Customer

Credibility
Concern
Competence

Emotional

Rational

Facts
Figures
Knowledge

Time

Closed-minded
Customer

Sale

a person who wants to truly understand their needs. You can stumble on some interesting data using the Internet. A sales superstar I know Googles his customers regularly. One time, to his dismay, he discovered that his customer had been hired by a competitor to speak at the competitor's annual corporate meeting!

Your research will help you ask well-thought-out, customized, well-researched questions (more on questioning techniques in chapter 4). Simply by showing that you have done your homework (research) and by asking powerful questions, you will gain customer trust and begin to understand your customer's world.

You can also gain credibility and show concern by helping customers with non-solution-specific information that helps them run their businesses better or avoid pain. This requires you to simply think about and uncover the pains that your customer may encounter before, during, and after he invests in your offering. For instance, if you were buying a home, a real estate agent might ask you a series of questions to fully understand your needs. Prior to showing you any homes, he might share information about moving companies, the community, favorite restaurants, schools, and public transportation. A commercial real estate agent might provide information on the local labor market, union penetration, or proximity to rail.

> **★ SUPERSTAR SECRET ★**
>
> **Gain initial trust by researching your customer, asking powerful questions, providing non-solution-specific information, and telling success stories.**

To increase your company's credibility in the customer's eyes, you might invite your customer to your office for a visit. You might use productivity analyses, industry benchmarking data, and your customer's own financial statements to gain credibility. Your company's marketing department should provide ready-made tools that you should know how to use, depending on your account's requirements. If your company doesn't provide these tools, you should create your own.

Success stories, or references, are another tool for gaining trust. Does your company have success stories to share? Typically, these are available through your company's marketing or service teams. If you can calculate specific customer savings, you can convincingly demonstrate proven achievements with the use of your solutions. Here's the best format for communicating success stories to your customers. Highlight four things: the customer, the challenge, the solution, and the results.

The best success story is a personal reference. A quick way to gain credibility is to point to someone else you have helped. The inference is that you have a track record that proves your knowledge and trustworthiness. You have consulted with others effectively, and you can help this customer as well.

How to Tell a Good Success Story

▶ **The Customer**
A large insurance company in the Midwest.

▶ **The Challenge**
The company's costs were rising faster than its revenue.

▶ **The Solution**
Implement enterprise-wide software to automate the management of all employee purchases and expenditures.

▶ **The Results**
A significant savings due to the elimination of rogue spending and off-contract buying. Estimated first-year savings: $5.4 million.

Don't Get Burned

Some sales reps don't want to take the time to climb the Trust Triangle. They say to themselves, "Why not take a shortcut and go horizontally from left to right?" Unfortunately, there is no straight line to a sale. And if you try, you will almost certainly get burned. The customer, put off by your pushy approach, will put you in the bucket with all the other stereotypical used-car salesman types. She'll stop listening and shut down, killing any chance of a sale.

Pitfalls of Attempting a Shortcut

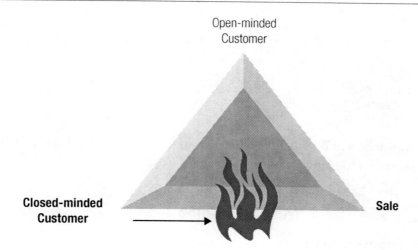

The Trust Triangle is always in flux. It is never fixed in shape or equilateral. With every sales situation it is configured differently, depending on where you are in the sales cycle and how your customer perceives you, your company, and your solution.

If there are significant barriers to trust, the climb up the left face of the Trust Triangle might look something like this:

Selling to a Suspicious Customer

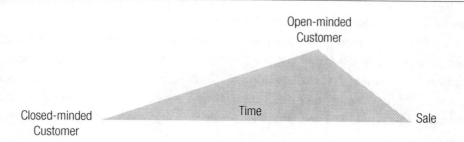

If, on the other hand, you've worked with the customer in the past and she has a high degree of trust in you, then you'll be rewarded with a short left face of the triangle and a short time span.

Selling to Your Mother

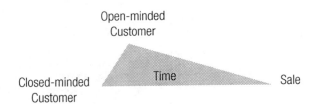

Each customer is different. Take whatever time is necessary to climb the left side of the triangle and gain trust.

▶ Trust Strategies ◀

I offer three sure-fire strategies for building trust:

- ▶ Never allow the customer to trip you up.
- ▶ Go to the first sales call naked.
- ▶ Send new account introduction letters.

Never Allow the Customer to Trip You Up

Earlier we discussed the importance of not jumping to the right-hand (rational) face of the triangle until you've climbed the left-hand (emotional) slope. But sometimes a customer herself will try to jump to the rational slope before you've had a chance to earn her trust or open her mind. She will stop you in the hallway and say something like, "Why should I buy your product? I've only got a minute."

If this happens to you, look out! This situation is a landmine. The customer is expecting you to talk really fast, back up the truck, and dump the data. Most reps, unfortunately, meet that expectation. They excitedly spew forth their marketing mantra, telling the customer that their solution is better, faster, and cheaper than anything else available. Moreover, the customer would be foolish to look at anyone else's product.

How presumptuous to push a solution without knowing whether it meets a need. Would you be comfortable buying from a rep who did that? I know I wouldn't. So how should you respond?

The correct answer to this customer's question would be, "That's a great question. However, without a full understanding of your specific needs and requirements, I really do not feel comfortable recommending why you should invest with us. Quite frankly, we may not be the right solution for you. Why don't we set next Friday as a tentative date to revisit that question? By then I will have had an opportunity to fully investigate and research your specific needs to determine if there is a fit between your needs and our solution. By the way, if there is not a good fit, I will be happy to assist you in working with another provider."

Remember what we said earlier: Superstars differentiate themselves not by *what* they sell but by *how* they sell. Your response will differentiate you from the typical sales professional and demonstrate your credibility and concern to the customer.

If the customer says, "But I only have a minute," you could say, "Your time is valuable. I don't want to waste it. First, I would like to see your system and the workflow in your department to see if it maps to our system. After that, *if* I believe that my solution can provide some benefit to you, I will follow up within a week, when you have more time."

Your goal is to establish long-term relationships with your customers and to manage your exchanges with integrity. Do not let the customer make you lose track of this.

Another way to get at this same point is to imagine yourself in your doctor's office. You're sitting on the crunchy white sheet of paper, looking at your watch, when the doctor strolls in and shakes your hand.

> *Doctor:* So, how are you feeling today?
>
> *You:* I'm not feeling very well, and I think a pain pill would help me.
>
> *Doctor:* Hmmm. Tell me more about how you're feeling.
>
> *You:* Doctor, I'm just asking for a pill.
>
> *Doctor:* Before I can tell you what's wrong and prescribe the correct medication, I have to first understand your concerns! Where do you have the worst pain? When did it start?

In other words, it is impossible for someone to begin solving a problem without a thorough understanding of the challenges and concerns behind the problem. Superstars, like doctors, should fully understand their customers' pain before talking about potential solutions.

The Naked Call

True or false: Always be prepared in your accounts for anything that the customer may throw at you. Bring as many resources as you can into each call. Superstars have a laser focus with customers and are begging to find reasons to visit an account repeatedly and regularly. They know that regular contact with the customer builds their credibility and gives them an opportunity to show their concern, therefore building trust.

What is a naked call? No, it's not what you think. When you walk into a customer's office for the first time, you want to make sure you are naked — that is, not dragging along tons of paraphernalia, such as a briefcase, films, laptop, and brochures. You do not want to be a detail rep. You've seen these guys. They bang through the customer's office doors with enough supplies to live on for a week. They've got a briefcase on a wagon with binders, papers, phones, and laptops.

What does a superstar bring into an account? A thin black leather folder with a pad of blank paper. Why? I want a reason to come back to that customer! I am hoping the customer wants something I don't have, so I can come back for another appointment to meet the request.

This is especially true when you bring your manager into an account. You may need to remind him that he is the big barking dog backing you up. Do you want him entering an account with all of his baggage? The truth is, you want him even more naked that you are. I have had to strip my managers and remind them that what I need from them is a big handshake, a nice suit, and a warm smile, along with their authority when I need it.

One of my managers joined me on a visit to the headquarters of one of the world's largest airlines. We were scheduled to meet with a senior executive about a multimillion-dollar software opportunity. I drove my manager to the location, parked the car, and my manager got out. I started walking toward the building when I heard the back car door open and close. I turned around to see that he had pulled out a huge briefcase stuffed with folders, binders, and a laptop computer. I quickly and politely reminded him of his role — he was a senior executive, and he needed to act the part. His role was to help me to gain trust by showing that our senior executives are committed to the customer relationship. His role was not to make a presentation or dump data on the customer. We agreed that at the very most he would bring one leather folder… and that I would be the one carrying it! I am glad to report that everything worked out well. We locked in a $5 million win.

The first trust strategy was to not allow customers to trip you up. The second was the naked call. Let's move on to the third strategy — using a new account introduction letter.

New Account Introduction Letter

What happens when you are assigned a brand-new account? You will quickly remember the trust formula: credibility, concern, and a little bit of competence. Do you walk into an account and announce, "Hey, dude, I'm your new rep"? You know better. The best way to introduce yourself is by drafting a letter for your

SECRET WEAPON 3

New Account Introduction Letter

Stuart Durkee
President
RJA Manufacturing Corp.
101 Cameron Road
Rice Lake, WI 54868

Dear Stuart:

I am pleased to announce that Benjamin Edwards will be your new Adams & Associates account manager.

Ben comes to Adams & Associates with an outstanding background that is a good match with the challenges facing your facility. After graduating with honors from Tulane with a BA in business administration, Ben went on to complete his MBA at Duke.

Ben's work experience includes outstanding performance at D&D (two years) and Alpha Corp (three years), where his customers appreciated both his in-depth product knowledge and consultative approach.

Ben has completed phase 1 of our rigorous training program and is up to date on all our products and solutions. Beyond simply providing equipment, he is very knowledgeable on the broad array of our offerings, including asset services, financial services, education services, and performance improvement services.

Ben and his wife, Amy, live in Eau Claire, where they are both avid golfers.

You should expect to receive a formal introduction from Ben within the next week. In the meantime, if you have any questions, you can reach him at 630-555-1212.

Sincerely,

Joe Feider
Sales Manager

manager (not you) to sign and send to the customer in advance. This is a great way to break the ice and establish credibility early on. The letter might look something like the one in **Secret Weapon 3.**

So let's say your manager sends out this letter on your behalf, and you're ready to march in and introduce yourself to the customer. What do you need to understand before you show up?

That's the focus of chapter 3.

CHAPTER THREE

INSIDE THE CUSTOMER BUYING PROCESS

▶ The Three Ds (D³) ◀

Companies spend boatloads of money teaching their reps the selling process, which is: qualify, uncover needs, present, handle objections, close. Those steps are important selling basics that will help you keep your job — they help you avoid "special assignment," otherwise known as being moved over and then out of the company. Each company modifies the selling process slightly, but all include the core components. The selling process also provides an important forecasting and tracking mechanism necessary to the health of your company, which is why we'll thoroughly go over it in chapter 4.

Trust Triangle Selling

Buyer

Decision Process | Buying Process

Seller

Superstar Selling Process

To be a superstar sales rep, however, you also need to understand your customer's buying process, which has very little to do with your company's internal selling process. The buying process is life from your customer's perspective.

★ SUPERSTAR SECRET ★

The rep who develops, documents, and drives the customer's buying process... *wins!*

Toward the end of my sales career I thought I knew it all. After joining Ariba I had the privilege of working for Mike Hills, a sharp manager with wisdom beyond his years. Mike, who hired me, eventually went on to become Ariba's General Manager of Europe and then National Sales Manager. I was sitting with him in his office one day, giving him an update on a major opportunity I was working on. I told him where we were in our sales process, went over all the important issues — budget, key players, funding, competition, purchase criteria — and addressed all his questions like a veteran rep should.

He asked a simple question that totally stopped me in my tracks: "What is their process?"

"Their process?" I said.

"Yeah, what is your customer's buying process from this point forward?"

In that one instant he shifted my focus from rep-centric to customer-centric. Since that day I have made it my business to understand the customer's buying process. I have refined Mike's insight into the following mantra: The rep who develops, documents, and drives the customer's buying process... *wins!*

Developing, documenting, and driving adds up to three Ds — I call them D-cubed, or D^3. They provide a vivid 3-D view of your customer. Follow those steps and you'll have deep insight into not just what your customers need but also how you can best help them achieve their goals.

▶ Developing the Process ◀

In the ideal situation the customer already has a clearly defined buying process with well-trodden stages. In that case the superstar's job is to uncover the process, document it, and drive it to a sale. In a complex sale, however, the customer typically does not possess deep insight into exactly what steps are required and what the timing of the steps should be, because he is not an expert. How many times in the past five years has the customer purchased a service or product like the one offered by the rep? Usually very few, if any. When the customer does not have an established buying process — which, with complex, high-end sales, is most of the time — the superstar's job, as a consultant, is to develop with the customer all the steps required to accomplish the goal.

If a customer balks at allowing me to assist him with any aspect of his buying process, I like to provide stories about how other customers have had to endure tremendous headaches when they moved forward without my assistance. I share the pain associated with not having a formal process, such as missed timetable commitments, wasted time, wasted money, incorrect solutions, long lead times, poor vendor conduct, and unprofessional results. Admittedly, I provide this service not just out of the goodness of my heart but in my own self-interest. But the customer truly needs sound advice. If you, as the superstar, don't supply it, who is the customer going to turn to?

> *Customer option 1:* Your customer hires an outside consultant to advise him on the purchase.
>
> *Customer option 2:* The customer turns to your competitor to serve as his trusted advisor.
>
> *Customer option 3:* Your customer decides to go it alone.

If your customer opts for any of the above, you as the sales rep are in big trouble. You have just been demoted from a superstar to a commodity. As we have touched on before, in the case of option 1, the outside consultant will act as an intermediary between you and your customer. The outside consultant will immediately block your access to the customer and control the information flow. It is impossible to gain trust through an intermediary.

If your customer doesn't hire an outside consultant but has not developed trust in you, he is likely to choose option 2 — and turn to your competitor, someone who has learned the importance of establishing trust and credibility and driving the buying process. In this case your *competitor* will act as your customer's inside consultant. Can you imagine a more humiliating scenario?

In the case of option 3 — your customer goes it alone — expect chaos.

If, on the other hand, a customer is entering unfamiliar territory — making a buying decision she has never before made and facing untold headaches as a result — imagine her relief when she encounters a trustworthy rep who says, "Ms. Customer, I've been down this road a million times. Allow me to hold your hand and show you the way. I know every rock in the road and I can prevent you from stumbling."

When I say to customers, "Please share with me the steps you plan to follow to get to your solution," many times the customers try to show off by reciting a long list. Most of the time they are wrong — they miss half the key steps. Why? As we said earlier, the customer seldom makes a major purchase such as this. There is no way she can be up to date on all the peculiarities of a major purchase, such as lead times, installation times, site preparation requirements, and training needs.

Benefits of Proper Account Guidance

If you learn to guide your accounts properly, you will reap many rewards. The proper account guidance:

▶ Permits you to properly qualify opportunities.

▶ Removes the hassle in setting up future sales calls. (No more "Hi, what's going on with your project?" phone calls.)

▶ Positions *you* as the customer's trusted consultant.

▶ Prevents the customer from hiring an outside consultant.

▶ Blocks your competitors from serving as the customer's trusted advisor.

▶ Allows you to guide, modify, and control the customer's buying process.

▶ Helps you select and deploy the proper strategy.

▶ Permits rock-solid forecasting! A rep with a command of D^3 who uses a compelling event time line (discussed below) to drive the sale is able to forecast accurately.

▶ Prevents surprises.

▶ Allows you to respond professionally to a sales manager who asks, "What can we do to close the account by the end of the week?"

▶ Increases the efficiency and effectiveness of the time you spend with the customer.

▶ Makes your customer look good in the eyes of his superiors.

The seven stages of the typical Customer Buying Process look like this:

1. Develop the corporate strategic plan.
2. Uncover needs and develop the business case.
3. Assess potential solutions.
4. Evaluate vendors.
5. Finalize vendor selection.
6. Implement or install the solution.
7. Gather user feedback.

The elapsed time between stages 1 and 7 can be weeks, months – even years, if the product or service is a major investment for the company. The difference between an average rep and a superstar sales rep is where in the process each of them comes on board. The average rep shows up midway through the process, around stage 4, the vendor-vetting stage, performing his dog-and-pony act at the appointed hour. A superstar sales rep, on the other hand, gets in on the ground floor – during the development of the corporate strategic plan. She is part of the process from the beginning, joining the customer conversation on day 1 – whether or not she has to help the customer develop the process.

Where You Enter the Customer Buying Process Is Key

★ **1 Superstar (early)** Develop the corporate strategic plan
  2 Uncover needs and develop the business case
  3 Assess potential solutions
▶ **4 Average Rep (late)** Evaluate vendors
  5 Finalize vendor selection
  6 Implement the solution
  7 Gather feedback

Regardless of the stage at which you enter the Customer Buying Process, you must uncover it. How do you do that? Simple. You ask. Sometimes it's as easy as that. If the customer is reticent, a quid pro quo approach can help. (Quid pro quo , which means "I do something for you – you do something for me," is discussed further in chapter 4.) You might say, "Ms. Customer, I would like to provide a presentation for you, but I could be much more helpful to you if I better understood your process." If you ask the customer to share her process and she claims she doesn't have one, that's a red flag. It could mean one of two things: (1) You are talking to the wrong person and need to be referred higher up in the organization, or (2) the company has never purchased such a product or service before and really does not have a process. In the latter case, it's an indication that the customer desperately needs help, whether or not she realizes it. Who is in the best position to assist her? You are! Time to step up and be a consultant to your customer.

Your job is to guide the customer along a mutually agreed upon pathway – not simply respond to customer demands. The relationship between superstar rep and customer can be likened to the cooperative relationship between a mountain guide and a novice mountaineer who are climbing Mount Everest together. The guide leads the way so the climber doesn't get lost or fall off a cliff. When the guide says "Climb on," the climber starts climbing. I need exactly that kind of cooperation from my customers.

If an inexperienced customer gets frightened or overexcited and pulls too hard on the rope, I don't want to be holding that rope and getting whipped around. As a younger rep with no experience, I got whipped around too many times by customers telling me to get them this quote, to go here, to go there. I was in reactive mode, whipping myself into a frenzy every time a customer made a demand. Don't allow your customers to jerk you off the mountain. Develop, document, and drive their buying process. Early on in their process, get them to sign on to a mutually agreed upon pathway. Giving them helpful guidance is much more enjoyable than getting rope burns.

But how do you do this? Let's imagine you are working with a customer and you say, "Pete, it would be helpful for me to understand your process for evaluating this major investment." And Pete responds, "That's a good question, but I don't know what my process is." If you're a young rep who doesn't know anything, you might make the mistake of saying, "Oh, OK. Next question." This customer is *begging* to run into a superstar.

A superstar would respond this way: "Well, you know what, Pete? In the past year I have assisted more than fifteen organizations in the seamless transition from planning, evaluating, acquisition, installation, and on through the effective use of the system. Let me share with you some of the templates we use to make this whole process very simple." If Pete says, "We're not ready to buy your product yet," the superstar says, "I'm offering this service to you not to get an order today, but to help. Buying such a large system can be full of hassles and headaches, and I know how to avoid them. I can make the whole process a breeze. I'm not asking you to buy. You're not ready to buy now, so how could I possibly ask you to buy my solution now? I'm simply here to offer my expertise as a consultant to walk you through this process. I worked with X, Y, and Z companies on just such a purchase. Let me share with you what really worked well for them." Customers find this to be an extremely compelling offer.

★ SUPERSTAR SECRET ★

You cannot influence what you do not know.

If your customer tells you he has a buying process but he is reluctant to share it, you can negotiate access to this information – again, via quid pro quo. If this seems like a lot of trouble, remember this: You cannot influence what you do not know. And if you have no influence, you are unlikely to win – and you probably are not a superstar. If you determine that you will never get access to the customer's buying process, you should use this information to help decide whether a Disengage strategy should be put into play (see Disengage Strategy, page 116). At a minimum you can use this information to properly qualify the opportunity (see Be My Perfect Cash Cow, page 94).

If your customer truly does not have a buying process, your job is to develop one in collaboration with the customer. If he does have an existing buying process, it will probably need modifying. In either case, as a superstar rep you help the customer by verifying dates, adding or removing steps, and offering your insights as a consultant.

If the customer has a buying process, you modify it as needed, adding dates and adding or removing steps – all in collaboration with the customer. You are the expert and since you have more experience in these sales than the customer, your

The Three Ds (D³)

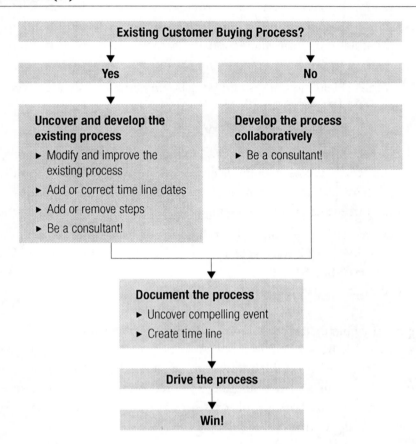

job is to help him. If the customer does *not* have a process, you develop one for the customer, documenting and driving the process to a win.

Compelling Event

Every Customer Buying Process is rooted in time. Toward the end of the process is a compelling event – a drop-dead date by which something must happen in order for the purchase to be a success. In the case of a breadwinner buying a life insurance policy, the compelling event would be the expiration date on the existing policy. Your customer might say, "Our funding runs out October 1," or "Our lease expires in April," or "Our first day of operation is July 15," or "If we don't fix this system by next Wednesday, I'll be fired." That's a pretty compelling event.

In the case of a family buying a new car, the compelling event might be an upcoming trip to Yosemite. The car must be purchased in time for the family to pack and leave. Most people buy a car once every five years. Within those same five years, the typical car salesperson has sold perhaps three hundred cars. So who knows more about cars and car buying? Unfortunately, few car salespeople are superstars who step up to the plate and really serve as consultants to their customers. If they did, their interactions with car buyers would go something like this:

> *Superstar:* Help me understand your buying criteria. What are you looking for?
>
> *Customer:* I'm looking for an SUV.
>
> *Superstar:* Great. There are several excellent manufacturers out there – Land Rover, Lexus, Honda, Mercedes-Benz, BMW, Volvo, Ford. Can you share with me the timing of your car investment and an idea of what price range you are looking at, so that I can begin to assist you?
>
> *Customer:* Sure. We would like to finalize our decision in the next two weeks. We need it for a vacation we are taking. And we would like to spend less than $40,000.
>
> *Superstar:* Great! Let me tell you how I can help.

The superstar would then share a *Consumer Reports* article that ranks all SUVs; share an unbiased article from J.D. Power and Associates on quality ratings for SUVs; share an unbiased article on the best way to negotiate the lowest finance rate for an auto loan; share information about the Costco Auto Program to ensure that the customer gets the best price; and advise the customer on how to blast through the abusive techniques that car salespeople too often use on customers.

"Wait!" you may be thinking, "no car salesperson *I* know would go to all this trouble or mention other manufacturers in a positive light." That's because few of them are superstars. A superstar would begin serving immediately as an unbiased consultant to the buyer. She would hand out *Consumer Reports* and the other quality ratings not to do a data dump of technical details (as I warned against earlier) but to provide a high-level overview of the various options. After all, the rep is still at the bottom left side of the Trust Triangle.

Compelling Event Time Line

The superstar sales rep helping the auto purchaser asked a key question: "What's your timing?" She uncovered the compelling event – the family's upcoming vacation. She would then create a time line of the many steps the customer will have to follow to ensure that he meets his two-week deadline. This time line outlines the customer's buying process.

Compelling Event Time Line

	Buying Process for Auto Purchase	Completion Date
1	Read articles provided by superstar sales rep.	
2	Visit BMW, Lexus, Honda, Volvo, Benz, Land Rover, Ford dealerships	
3	Narrow vendors down to three, based on initial impressions.	
4	Sign up for the Costco Auto Program.	
5	Contact three banks to inquire about financing rates.	
6	Select vehicle.	
7	Secure financing.	
8	Negotiate purchase price with dealer.	
9	Finalize agreement and pick up SUV.	
10	Leave for vacation.	(Compelling event)

Each step has a corresponding date by which the action must be accomplished in order for the project to be completed on time. It might surprise you to see visiting other dealerships as step 2 on the list. Would any car salesperson you know send you across the street to the competition? Again, a superstar would. She knows that there is much more to be gained by breaking out of the mold of a traditional rep and by serving as a true consultant to her customers. She also realizes that you are probably going to check out the dealership across the street anyway.

Another analogy is to imagine yourself as a travel consultant who is helping a customer plan an important trip. You would provide account guidance by determining his destination, the reason for the trip, and his required arrival time; reviewing with him the fastest and most scenic routes; mapping out the best route for his specific needs, turn by turn; and routinely checking in with the driver to ensure that he is not lost and that he is on target to reach his destination on time. If we translated that guidance into the principles of D^3, it would look like the exhibit on the next page.

By definition, a compelling event *must* be tied to a specific date. It cannot be something like, "We must buy this system in early autumn." That is too vague and will provide no help to you or your customer. I like to think of the compelling event as something that will cause great pain in the customer's world if action is not taken by a specific date.

What should you do if your customer does not have an obvious compelling event? You create one. As a consultative sales rep it is your job to educate the customer on the pain associated with not moving forward on a project by a specific date. It

D³ Account Guidance

Travel Consultant Steps	D³ Steps
▶ Determine the traveler's destination, reason for the trip, and required arrival date.	▶ Uncover the compelling event.
▶ Review with him the fastest and most scenic routes.	▶ Develop the process.
▶ Map out the best route for his specific needs, turn by turn.	▶ Document the process using the compelling event time line.
▶ Routinely check in with the driver to ensure that he is not lost and that he is on target to reach his destination on time.	▶ Drive the process.

could be financial pain, regulatory pain, or the pain caused by the competition gaining a first-mover advantage. Sometimes you can perform a return on investment (ROI) calculation whose object is to define a compelling event. You may be able to demonstrate the financial impact of delaying a purchase by saying to the customer, for example, "Every day you put off this project is costing your business $182,000." When discussing the compelling event with the customer, make sure that she agrees with and owns this date. Any date you alone present is irrelevant.

What happens if you still cannot come up with a compelling event? Does that mean you should use a Disengage strategy and abandon the opportunity? Probably not. But I can guarantee you one thing: The chance of your winning the deal decreases drastically, and you can forget trying to forecast this one. It's almost impossible. The customer has no real reason to move on the sale, and will always find some reason to delay.

★ SUPERSTAR SECRET ★

Keep an eye out for STPs – superstar turning points. These are chances for you to stop and think, and then choose to be a consultant.

Once you have the compelling event it is time to marry it to the various buying process steps and construct a time line. Who is in the very best position to begin consulting with the customer on uncovering the compelling event and creating the time line? Who knows best how much time to allow for delivery, installation, testing, and training? This opportunity is another superstar turning point, or STP – a chance for you to stop and think, and then choose to be a consultant. No one knows the buying process better than the superstar!

Note: Do not use the term *compelling event* with customers – it is for internal use only. When I'm talking with customers I call the compelling event "your deadline" and I call the time line their "project timetable" or "process for purchasing."

► Documenting the Process ◄

The superstar should carry the burden of documenting the customer's buying process, creating a paper trail of what has happened so far and what needs to happen in the future. Why go to all this trouble to map out the process for customers? Why not just sell the goods and let the customer worry about time lines and such? You might say to yourself, "Some of this makes sense, but I haven't really felt the need to get so involved in their process. I do fine just responding with bids."

First, if you don't get involved early, you may miss out. In fact, you may have missed out already, but just don't know it. If a sales rep misses the opportunity to develop, document, and drive the customer's buying process, the customer may feel the need to hire an outside consultant to help her. After all, your customer is exposed. When a business is faced with the daunting task of investing a significant amount of money without a formalized process in place, it becomes a major headache maker. Remove the need for an outside consultant by stepping up for your customer.

Second, in complex, high-end sales, the customer's project is unlikely to succeed without your help. As a superstar rep your job is to be a consultant to the customer, guiding her every step of the way.

Third, the person documenting the process has a measure of control over the process. With every choice of word and every date on the time line you are setting the terms for the discussion, providing structure, and managing customer expectations. The customer wants to get somewhere. Your job is to draw a clear map.

At every step in the customer's buying process you will be generating paper. Together, these letters, tables, and Gantt charts are known as process documents. Process documents move the process along and create a written history of the sale. This history can be useful if disruptions derail the time line and the customer needs to understand the cause of the derailment.

Process documents help you determine how long a project should take, lay out the order of tasks, manage the dependencies among the tasks, determine the resources needed, monitor project progress, and take remedial action, if necessary, to get the project back on track. Throughout the book you'll find samples of the process documents I've used over the years – my secret weapons. They range from simple and straightforward to detailed and complex. Feel free to adapt them to your needs. Take the time to make your process documents visually appealing; they are a reflection of your professionalism and your high regard for your customer.

Secret Weapon 4 is a very simple process letter that documents the superstar's first meeting with the customer and outlines the next steps.

One of the next process documents the superstar sales rep generates for the client is a time line, or buying process. **Secret Weapons 5 through 9** show various

SECRET WEAPON 4

Simple Process Letter

Stuart Durkee
President
RJA Manufacturing Corp.
101 Cameron Road
Rice Lake, WI 54868

Dear Stuart:

Thank you for meeting with me today to discuss the System Upgrade Project. You confirmed that your primary issue is declining department revenue due to inadequate capacity. You indicated that Jim Thompson and his team could increase capacity with a new system.

We've agreed that the next step is for me to provide a detailed assessment of your existing systems so that we can develop a strategic plan for the whole department.

I will call your office on Friday to set up a meeting in two weeks, at which time I will share my findings.

Sincerely,

Ben

Benjamin Edwards

cc: Jim Thompson

SECRET WEAPON 5

Buying Process: Table Format

Task	Start Date	Suspense Date	Requirement	Action	Assigned To	Status	Comments
1	2 Aug	5 Aug	Gain agreement on remaining steps	Creation of a time line through Go Live and Phase 1	Kristine, Jack	Complete	
2	5 Aug	5 Aug	Collect pricing metrics	Users, employees, volumes, confirm modules	Jack, Kristine	Complete	
3	5 Aug	8 Aug	Request hosting estimate	Request hosting estimate	Jack	Complete	
4	10 Aug	10 Aug	Refinement of gap services scope	Meeting at ABC to review service requirements	ABC, Keisha, Jack, Mohammed	*Past due*	
19	5 Sep	5 Sep	Technical implementation kickoff	Kickoff	TSC, Dana	Not started	
20	7 Oct	14 Oct	ABC team formal training	Training in training center or on-site delivery	Jack, Kristine, Maura C.	Not started	Most likely in Miami with a GSO orientation
21	3 Aug	31 Oct	Go Live	Go Live	Dana	Not started	
22	1 Nov	31 Jan	Delivery of fall programs	Sourcing of fall programs	ABC, Adams	Not started	Rfx creation in Nov. Bidding in Dec. and Jan.

ways to lay out a buying process. All have been taken from real-world selling situations but are generic enough to be used in almost any major selling scenario. **Secret Weapon 5,** Buying Process: Table Format, is a simple one-page table of each task's start and end dates, owner, and current status.

The Customer Buying Process can be very complicated; the superstar's job is to simplify it for the customer. **Secret Weapon 6** is a simplified version of a time line I created for a global food company. Composing this time line provided several benefits. First, it helped the customer, who hadn't thought about making a time line, establish a process. It made his job easier and enhanced his competence in the eyes of his manager. Second, it helped me gain credibility, since I was able to help the customer establish a structure for his buying process. Together we thought of things he hadn't thought of before, such as the need to assign project teams, develop specifications, and organize the vendor selection process. Finally, it helped me guide the customer and drive the process along with him. On different occasions I would call to mention an upcoming deadline and remind him of the need for a formal presentation and demonstration. This time line helped me in a variety of ways to close the deal.

Secret Weapon 7, which is more complicated, shows the evaluation process for a company considering a major purchase, laid out on a calendar. **Secret Weapon 8,** Buying Process: Column Format, includes the action items along with the owner and expected duration of each item. In **Secret Weapon 9,** Buying Process: Gantt Chart Format, the tasks are mapped to weeks.

SECRET WEAPON 6

Buying Process: Time Line Format

Jan	Feb	Mar	Apr	May	Jun	Jul	Aug	Sep	Oct	Nov	Dec
Need identified	Feasibility study	Business case	Business case presented	Project team assigned	Potential solutions identified	Potential vendors selected	Specifications developed	RFP	Vendor selection	Final negotiations	Installation and implementation

SECRET WEAPON 7

Buying Process: Calendar Format

Instructions

▶ On the left-hand side, make notes about your project or event.

▶ Then, when you have entered the title and dates for each phase of your event or project, shade the dates on the calendar to correspond with the dates for your event or project.

▶ To shade dates on the calendar, select the dates you want to shade. Then, on the Format menu, click Borders and Shading, and then click the Shading tab. Choose the color you want, and then click OK.

200X

	January	February	March
	1 2 3 4 5 6 7	1 2 3 4	1 2 3 4
	8 9 10 11 12 13 14	5 6 7 8 9 10 11	5 6 7 8 9 10 11
	15 16 17 18 19 20 21	12 13 14 15 16 17 18	12 13 14 15 16 17 18
	22 23 24 25 26 27 28	19 20 21 22 23 24 25	19 20 21 22 23 24 25
	29 30 31	26 27 28	26 27 28 29 30 31

	April	May	June
	1	1 2 3 4 5 6	1 2 3
	2 3 4 5 6 7 8	7 8 9 10 11 12 13	4 5 6 7 8 9 10
	9 10 11 12 13 14 15	14 15 16 17 18 19 20	11 12 13 14 15 16 17
	16 17 18 19 20 21 22	21 22 23 24 25 26 27	18 19 20 21 22 23 24
	23 24 25 26 27 28 29	28 29 30 31	25 26 27 28 29 30
	30		

	July	August	September
	1	1 2 3 4 5	1 2
	2 3 4 5 6 7 8	6 7 8 9 10 11 12	3 4 5 6 7 8 9
	9 10 11 12 13 14 15	13 14 15 16 17 18 19	10 11 12 13 14 15 16
	16 17 18 19 20 21 22	20 21 22 23 24 25 26	17 18 19 20 21 22 23
	23 24 25 26 27 28 29	27 28 29 30 31	24 25 26 27 28 29 30
	30 31		

	October	November	December
	1 2 3 4 5 6 7	1 2 3 4	1 2
	8 9 10 11 12 13 14	5 6 7 8 9 10 11	3 4 5 6 7 8 9
	15 16 17 18 19 20 21	12 13 14 15 16 17 18	10 11 12 13 14 15 16
	22 23 24 25 26 27 28	19 20 21 22 23 24 25	17 18 19 20 21 22 23
	29 30 31	26 27 28 29 30	24 25 26 27 28 29 30
			31

Project/Event Name

Organizer's Name

Project Phase	Starting	Ending
Phase 1	01/27/0X	02/10/0X
Phase 2	02/13/0X	03/31/0X
Phase 3	04/03/0X	04/21/0X
Checkpoint	05/17/0X	

SECRET WEAPON 8

Buying Process: Column Format

Project

Prepared By

Date

Although this looks like an internal document for a sales rep, it is actually the customer's buying process, documented by the superstar in collaboration with the customer and given to the customer.

General Info

Customer Name:

Address:

City, State:

Main Number:

Bed Size: Corp Acct:

Installation

First Use Date:

Account Profile:

Economic Criteria:

Technical Criteria:

User Criteria:

ID	Action Item	Owner	Duration
	Project kickoff	Project Champion	1 day
	Agree on decision process		
	Agree on decision team		
	Identify project goals		
	Needs analysis	Decision Team	14 days
	Understand user needs and priorities		
	Understand economic needs and priorities		
	Compile requirements document		
	Solutions overview and demo	Decision Team	14 days
	Solution presentation		
	Demonstration of solution to meet needs		
	Confirm solution meets needs		
	User due diligence	User Team	1/2 day
	Review to ensure technologists' satisfaction		
	Technical due diligence	Technical Team	1/2 day
	Review to ensure doctors' satisfaction		
	Economic due diligence	Economic Buyer	3 days
	Compile spend data		
	Complete detailed project ROI analysis		
	Reference calls	Decision Team	2 days
	Provide reference lists for candid questions		
	Executive sponsorship *(optional)*	Administration	1 day
	Overview and demonstration		
	Session with corporate account team		
	Legal	Legal	14 days
	Secure legal approvals		
	Contact completion		
	Purchasing agreement	Economic and Purchasing	5 days
	Review project proposal		
	Finalize business terms		
	Sign license and service agreement		
	Issue purchase order		
	Implementation	Decision Team	
	Exceeding expectations meeting		1 day
	Site readiness		5 days
	Installation		14 days
	First use		1 day

SECRET WEAPON 9

Buying Process: Gantt Chart Format

This Gantt chart is created by the superstar sales rep in collaboration with the customer and kept updated by the rep.

	Action Item	Week											
		1	2	3	4	5	6	7	8	9	10	11	12
1	Agree on decision process.	•											
2	Agree on makeup of decision team.	•											
3	Complete generic technical specifications.		•										
4	Vendors receive sample generic technical specifications for feedback.		•										
5	Receive vendor feedback on generic technical specifications.		•										
6	Finalize formal bid specifications.			•									
7	Vendors receive bid specifications.			•									
8	Vendors submit questions via e-mail.				•								
9	Vendors receive detailed responses to questions.				•								
10	Vendors provide formal responses to bid request.					•							
11	Write script for reference calls.					•							
12	Call references.						•						
13	Summarize reference responses.						•						
14	**Adams & Associates provides detailed bid analysis and executive summary.**							•					
15	Ginger, Manuel, Kristina, and doctors develop one-page demonstration script.					•							
16	**Vendor Report Card developed for Demo Day.**						•						
17	Vendors receive demonstration script.						•						
18	Vendors demonstrate solution following demonstration script during 4-hour Demo Day.								•				
19	Staff completes Report Card on the scripted demonstration for each vendor.								•				
20	Summarize Report Card information.								•				
21	Vendors invited to final negotiation.									•			
22	Negotiations take place.										•		
23	**Negotiation summary developed by Adams and Associates.**										•		
24	Prepare high-level summary of bid response; evaluate Demo Day; develop final negotiation.										•		
25	Finalize vendor selection and notify vendors.										•		
26	**Installation begins July 31.**												•

In item 14, the superstar sales rep, working on the inside as the customer's consultant, provides a detailed analysis of all vendor bids, including his own.

In item 16, the superstar sales rep develops this presentation report card for the client. See Secret Weapon 11, Presentation Report Card.

In item 23, the negotiation summary developed by the superstar rep includes his figures plus those of all competitors.

In item 26, the compelling event (installation) begins during a company-observed vacation.

Note the level of detail in the documents. Are you confused by the internal look of some of them, particularly Secret Weapons 7 and 8? When consulting on high-end sales, the superstar rep is very much *inside* the customer's company, documenting the buying process as a consultant on behalf of the customer. That's why I call them secret weapons – because in most cases the competition does not know that you are serving as the trusted consultant to the customer.

The buying process road map is a living, breathing document that is reviewed with the customer at the beginning and end of each sales call. At the beginning you use the road map to verify that you and your customer are still on schedule and that nothing has changed. At the end of the sales call you again review the document with the customer to ensure that all the next steps and action items are set and agreed upon. The road map often requires adjustment. You, as the superstar, are responsible for the modifications; you should continually give the customer current copies of the updated process.

There are several ways to construct a time line and document the customer's buying process. You can use a complex software program, a simple printed calendar, or just a one-page letter. Choose a format that fits well with how you think, how your customer thinks, and how your industry works. No matter what you use, just be sure you document your time line. It should be clearly understandable and easy to read and it should accurately reflect your customer's requirements.

★ SUPERSTAR SECRET ★

Provide templates to help the customer document every stage of the buying process.

Throughout the customer's buying process you continue to provide documentation. **Secret Weapons 10, 11, 12, and 13** are buying process documents typically used by customers during the Evaluate Vendors stage. The customer either generates the documents on his own – or, if a superstar is involved – adapts them from a template provided by the superstar. Remember what we said earlier: Most customers buying complex, high-end hardware or software systems have never handled such a sale before and have limited knowledge about how to proceed. You, as the superstar who has gone through this process many times before, can help the customer enormously by providing the right tools at the right moments. This will save both you and your customer lots of time and headaches.

These secret weapons can be confusing to reps unfamiliar with high-end sales and the depth to which the superstar is involved in the customer organization. "Wait a minute!" they think. "The superstar is giving the customer the template of a letter that the customer will then send *back* to the superstar?" Yes. That's how involved you will get. And the other vendors will not realize the extent of your involvement.

SECRET WEAPON 10

Presentation Protocol Letter

CORPORATION

Dear [Vendor]:

Thank you for agreeing to present your solution to our staff on February 23.

Below is the required presentation format for all participants. Failure to adhere to this agenda and time line will result in your elimination from our decision process.

You will have one hour to provide the following presentation:

Agenda Item	Minutes
Introduction	5
Corporate overview	10
Suggested solution	20
Works in progress	10
Questions and answers	15

> To produce this letter, which describes the protocol for the vendor presentations, the customer, Lee, borrows a template from the superstar.

Please contact Andrea Brinks at 555-1212 if you have any questions. We look forward to your presentation.

Sincerely,

Lee Gannon
Senior Vice President

cc: Alice Murphy, MD

SECRET WEAPON 11

Presentation Report Card

To make it easier for the customer to evaluate the vendor presentations, the superstar provides this report card.

Solution Criteria	1 Poor	2	3 Average	4	5 Excellent

Solution Criteria	Grade	Comments
Training	4	Last year they were still in a learning curve. Training is now excellent.
Professionalism	3	Started late.
Ease of use; minimal learning curve	3	Buttons not large enough.
Reliability	2	Not a great reputation on this.
Upgradeability; adaptability to future technology	4	
Long-term corporate viability	3	
Service and support – Hardware service – Software service	 4 4	Most of the time does a great job. Sometimes calling them is like calling the IRS. Service guys are engineer-specific.
References	1	No others using this system at this date.
Overall satisfaction	4	

SECRET WEAPON 12

Request for Proposal Cover Letter

CORPORATION

Deadline for Questions: 5:00 p.m. CST, Friday, May 9
Deadline for Proposals: 5:00 p.m. CST, Friday, May 23

Jane McWilliams
Sales Manager
Technology Partners
14 Robinson Hill Road
Maple Corner, VT 05648

> **In this letter the customer invites the three or so vendors who successfully made it through the initial presentation process to now make a formal proposal.**

Dear Jane:

Thank you very much for the hard work and effort you put into assisting our team with the selection of our new software solution.

We have narrowed our software vendors to three. We would appreciate it if you would respond to the attached Request for Proposal. Please submit your formal proposal to lee@abccorporation.com no later than *5:00 p.m. CST, Friday, May 23*. Proposals received after that time will not be accepted.

The process we have put in place ensures an equitable evaluation of each vendor's offerings. If you have any questions regarding these specifications, please direct them to me at lee@abccorporation.com no later than *5:00 p.m. CST, Friday, May 9*. I will summarize the questions and respond to all vendors via e-mail. Note: questions received after that date will not be answered.

Please make a note on your calendar that on the morning of *Friday, June 13*, the successful vendors from our proposal process will be invited to participate in a software demonstration at our offices.

Thanks in advance for your participation in our evaluation.

Sincerely,

Lee

> **This letter is among the templates the superstar offers to the customer, if the customer needs it.**

Lee Gannon
Senior Vice President

SECRET WEAPON 13

Request for Proposal Excerpt

> During the Evaluate Vendors stage of the Customer Buying Process, the customer sends this RFP to potential vendors.

> Some customers have never before put together an RFP. If so, you, as the superstar, can provide a template. Adapt this RFP to your industry.

Software Solution
Request for Proposal

Section 1: Vendor Instructions
Section 2: Decision Criteria
Section 3: Formal Proposal Format
Section 4: Detailed Software Requirements
Section 5: Detailed Hardware Requirements
Section 6: Vendor Contact Information
Section 7: Financial Information
Section 8: Your Competitive Advantage
Section 9: Experience and References
Section 10: Resources Required
Section 11: Training

Section 12: Software and Hardware Upgrades
Section 13: HIPAA
Section 14: Warranty, Maintenance, and Support
Section 15: Maintenance and Support Pricing
Section 16: Quotation Options
Section 17: Solution Pricing
Section 18: Payment Terms
Section 19: Source Code Protection
Section 20: Performance Guarantee
Section 21: Authorized Signature

Section 1: Vendor Instructions

Deadline

Please submit your formal written response to this proposal request no later than *5:00 p.m. CST, Friday, May 23*. Proposals received after that cut-off will not be accepted.

Definitions

► *Software Vendor:* The vendor responsible for the design and manufacture of the software.

► *Reseller:* The vendor responsible for the sale, distribution, installation, and implementation of the Software Vendor's solution.

► *Hardware Vendor:* The vendor responsible for the manufacture of the proposed hardware.

Questions

The process we have put in place ensures an equitable evaluation of each vendor's offerings. If you have any questions regarding these specifications, please direct them to lee@abccorporation.com no later than *5:00 p.m. CST, Friday, May 9*. I will summarize the questions and respond to all vendors via e-mail. Note: questions received after that date will not be answered.

SECRET WEAPON 13 (continued)

Request for Proposal Excerpt

Section 2: Decision Criteria

Our selection of a vendor will be based on how well the solution addresses the following:

- ▸ Total cost of ownership (TCO)
- ▸ Reliability
- ▸ Service and support
- ▸ Administrative and clinical functionality
- ▸ Ease of use; minimal learning curve

Vendor Response

Please use blue font and use as much space as necessary.

Section 3: Formal Proposal Format

For ease of reading, we request that all proposals follow this format and include specific discounted line item prices.

Part A

- ▸ System software
- ▸ Fiscal financial software (payroll, P&L, balance sheet, general ledger)
- ▸ Financial accounts receivable
- ▸ Schedule
- ▸ Clinical and charting
- ▸ Other

Part B

- ▸ Site preparation
- ▸ Installation
- ▸ Maintenance, support, and upgrades

Part C

Instructor-led training (including *all* travel costs)

> Since the customer, Lee, has never before sent out a detailed RFP, he borrows a template from our superstar, Ben. Ben is able to advise Lee about the process and the need for clear deadlines.

The conversation with the customer about the templates should be relaxed and easy. You ask, "Have you gone through this step before?" If the answer is no, you continue: "Would you like to see how I've handled this with other customers in the past?" You will probably see a very relieved expression on the customer's face.

Secret Weapon 10 is a letter in which a customer, Lee Gannon, communicates to vendors the required format for their upcoming presentations. The customer has never before set up presentations like this, so he borrows a template from our superstar, Ben. Ben advises Lee as to the suggested agenda and timing. **Secret Weapon 11** is a report card on which Lee and his colleagues make notes about each vendor presentation — again, provided by Ben. Ben provides enough report cards for Lee and his colleagues to evaluate all three vendors.

After the presentations, Lee, the customer, narrows down the field of possible vendors to three or four and invites them to submit formal proposals. If the customer needs help with this (and many do!), the superstar again steps in with the necessary templates. **Secret Weapon 12** is the request for proposal (RFP) cover letter. **Secret Weapon 13** is an excerpt from a detailed RFP. In both, note the two-week lag between the question cut-off and the submission cut-off. Ben, who has been part of this process a hundred times, is protecting the customer from the annoyance of last-minute questions. Note also how, in the template, Lee promises to share the answers to every vendor question with *all* vendors, out of fairness to all.

The Customer Buying Process and templates shown here are not set in stone. Each was invented to prevent chaos and pain for both the customer and rep. For example, a lack of generic bid specifications can cause pricing chaos later, with the buyer basing the purchase only on initial selling price without looking at the return on investment (ROI) or total cost of ownership (TCO). Or the purchase is based on price, but the quotations are not apples-to-apples, and one vendor's solution provides three times the capability or features of the low-priced winner.

Adapt the templates in Secret Weapons 10 through 13 to your industry, print them out on plain white paper, and keep them in a binder, ready to review with customers when they need them. (We will return to these secret weapons again in chapter 4, in the sales process step Providing Proof and Justification.)

Now that we've explored the first two Ds in D^3 — discover and document — let's turn to the third and perhaps most important D, at least philosophically: *driving* the process toward completion.

SECRET WEAPON 14

Mutual Memo of Understanding

Stuart Durkee
President
RJA Manufacturing Corp.
101 Cameron Road
Rice Lake, WI 54868

Dear Stuart:

RJA Manufacturing Corporation and Adams & Associates will be exchanging information with one another throughout the evaluation stage of the System Upgrade Project.

In the event that either party believes that the information shared is confidential or proprietary, the parties agree to enter into a nondisclosure agreement.

I am looking forward to working with you on this project. In recognition of our mutual understanding, please sign the bottom of this letter and return it to me.

Please contact me with any questions or concerns.

Sincerely,

Ben

Benjamin Edwards

cc: Jim Thompson

_____

Stuart Durkee

► Driving the Process ◄

It is important to understand the customer's compelling event so that you can guide the customer in a direction that is mutually beneficial, in this case staying on track with his buying process. If you try to schedule a product demonstration and the customer balks, you can suggest, "If we are going to make our deadline of October 1, we will need to set up the demo now." This all contributes to the superstar's ability to drive the Customer Buying Process.

Mutual Memo of Understanding

A mutual memo of understanding (MMOU) – **Secret Weapon 14** – is a simple letter that protects the confidentiality of information shared between you and the customers. The word *mutual* is critical; it emphasizes that the agreement protects both parties – yes, the MMOU protects both you and the customer – from disclosures that could be detrimental. From the superstar's perspective, however, the MMOU has an even more powerful use: It signals the customer's willingness to be guided. Typically, the MMOU is one of the first steps in the Customer Buying Process. After you explain its importance to the customer, she usually puts it near the beginning of her time line. If she balks at signing this simple letter, what are the odds that she will allow you to guide her down the path? The customer's reaction will indicate how difficult the job will be. It is also a way to encourage the customer to walk along with you; it starts driving the process.

Early in the process an MMOU works better than a formal mutual nondisclosure agreement (MDA or MNDA) precisely because it is so informal and therefore easier for the customer to swallow. A nondisclosure agreement is typically a lengthy, complicated document that can delay the process if introduced in the initial stages. In addition, the MMOU serves as a soft warning to the customer that a more formal nondisclosure agreement may be necessary later on, depending on the customer situation.

"I Don't Have Time"

After most reps are exposed to the concepts in this chapter, the light goes on and they begin to understand the power of D^3 – developing, documenting, and driving the customer's buying process. A few, however, say to themselves, "That's really nice, but I don't have time to do that." They think it increases the time they need to dedicate to the customer. This is not true. The unintended consequences of letting the customer drive the process are chaos and wasted time. Yes, with each major opportunity you will have to do some extra work to drive the process. But the time you spend will be more than offset by the time you save later on. Ask successful

Increasing Your Chances of Winning

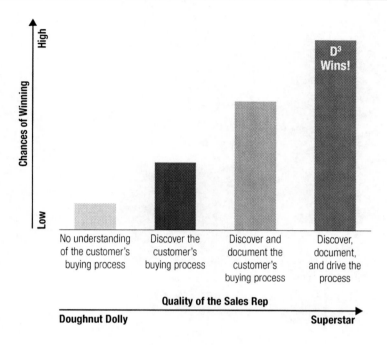

sales reps what it is like to work with a customer who has no buying process. They will share many examples of how time was wasted due to rebidding, duplicative presentations, and multiple demonstrations. Upfront work eliminates chaos later.

To summarize, you'll discover numerous benefits to D^3. If those benefits aren't reason enough to bother taking the time, consider this: Your chances of success increase dramatically with every step you take.

For the past three chapters we have sat on the customer's side of the table, trying to understand life from his point of view. In chapter 4 we make a dramatic shift to the superstar sales rep's point of view. We'll borrow a theme from the oldest military treatise in the world, *The Art of War* by Sun Tzu, who advises maneuvering in such a way that the other party (or, in this case, the customer) can do *only* what you want him to do — and that he does so willingly. In our case, since we are not at war with the customer, this means moving cooperatively and collectively with the customer — at times responding, at times guiding — each walking with a common purpose, in a direct line toward the sale.

CHAPTER FOUR

MASTERING THE SUPERSTAR SELLING PROCESS

I stumbled a lot when I first began selling. It took me a while to understand my company's selling process, the customer's decision process, the customer's buying process, and how all these processes mesh. Put together, the processes form a three-legged stool — solid and stable if all three legs are there, but fragile if one is missing. Before I understood and mastered all three legs, I frequently crashed to the floor. Sometimes I focused on the needs of my selling process at the expense of my customers' needs; for instance, I'd push information on them before they

Trust Triangle Selling

Buyer
Decision Process | Buying Process
Seller
Superstar Selling Process

were ready to listen, and lose credibility. Other times I focused too exclusively on the customer's needs and forgot the needs of my company, spending too many resources on prospects who were unlikely to buy.

The key is to remember that while you're following the steps in the superstar selling process you are also climbing the left side of the Trust Triangle. And while you're busy building credibility, showing concern, and thinking about which secret weapon to deploy and when, the customer is making decisions emotionally and justifying them rationally. Keeping all three processes in mind is like watching three TV monitors simultaneously. With some luck, and if you do your job well, eventually all three screens display the same image: you and the customer working together toward a mutually beneficial end. The Customer Buying Process, which includes the Customer Decision Process, must always take the lead. The superstar guides the Customer's Buying Process using D^3 (see chapter 3) and the Superstar Selling Process.

Superstar Selling Process

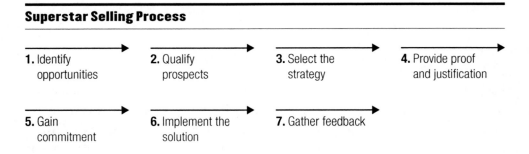

1. Identify opportunities
2. Qualify prospects
3. Select the strategy
4. Provide proof and justification

5. Gain commitment
6. Implement the solution
7. Gather feedback

The superstar selling process has seven steps. The first five − (1) identifying opportunities, (2) qualifying prospects, (3) selecting the strategy, (4) providing proof and justification, and (5) gaining commitment − take you through the moment the contract is signed. After the deal is sealed, the process continues with (6) implementing the solution and (7) gathering feedback. These seven steps are not carved in stone. At your company the steps may be called something different, the steps might be combined, or even expanded into more detail. The basic concepts are similar. Do not confuse these steps with the facts, figures, and knowledge you share as you descend the right side of the Trust Triangle toward a sale.

▶ Step 1 — Identifying Opportunities ◀

Prospecting can be one of the most arduous parts of a superstar's job. It is crucial, however, to the long-term success of any territory and business. Much of the discomfort that usually goes along with prospecting can be eliminated by developing a routine or process, which I call the Prospecting Machine. But first things first: before you can approach customers, you need to know what you're selling. Let's talk about value propositions and research.

Value Proposition

A value proposition is not a thing, like a product or a service. It's a sales message that shows that you thoroughly understand the following:

- ▶ Who the customer is and the exact nature of his or her headaches
- ▶ How your product or solution can eliminate or prevent those headaches and provide desired benefits
- ▶ The ways in which you are uniquely qualified to do this
- ▶ Justification for why a customer should invest more for your solution
- ▶ Proof that you can do it

In short, your value proposition answers the customer question, "Why should I buy from you?" As much as we'd prefer otherwise, the answer is never because we're good looking or we deserve a break today. The answer must always boil down to, "Because it's in the customer's best interests to do so." Your value proposition *proves* this.

Preparing and internalizing an effective value proposition is one of the very first things a rep should do upon joining a company. Preferably, the value proposition is developed in conjunction with senior executives and corporate marketing. It

Components of a Value Proposition

Component	Answer This Customer Question
The Promise	"How can you help me?"
The Enablers	"What is the arsenal of services, technologies, products, and solutions that allow you to make the commitment to me?"
The Unfair Advantage	"What makes you different from your competition?"
The Justification	"Why, specifically, should I invest more for your offering than the competition's?"
The Proof	"I don't believe you — prove it."

should take into account the overall corporate strategic direction. Everyone from the person who answers the phones to the CxO to the janitorial staff should know the company's value proposition. Although you must memorize it, you will never use your value proposition in its entire memorized form with a customer. Let me repeat, you will *never* use your value proposition in its memorized form. You customize it to each customer based on his or her specific role. A rep who uses the value proposition without customization is signaling to the customer that the rep does not care enough about the customer to invest the time to learn about the customer's specific needs and business vulnerabilities. A powerful value proposition has five components: The promise, the enablers, the unfair advantage, the justification, and the proof.

> ★ SUPERSTAR SECRET ★
>
> **Your value proposition should provide a clear, compelling answer to the question, "Why should I buy from you?"**

THE PROMISE

This first value proposition component answers the customer question, "How can you help me?" The promise is your high-level commitment to an account to help it succeed. Typically, your commitment will be to help the customer reduce costs, increase revenue, increase efficiency, improve quality, or strengthen its market position. These are your high-level promises. Promises are not the same as benefits. If you were selling refrigerators, your promise would not be to keep a family's food at a consistent forty degrees Fahrenheit; your promise would be to help maintain everyone's good health and improve the quality of the family's life. If you were selling medical billing software, your promise would not be the software's ability to print labels at top speed; it would be to reduce billing costs and improve the hospital's bottom line.

THE ENABLERS

The second component of your value proposition answers the customer question, "What arsenal of services, technologies, products, and solutions allow you to make the promise to me?" The enablers are what you offer to fulfill the promise. For example, if your promise to the customer is, "I can help you increase revenue," the enablers explain the tools, solutions, services, and technologies you offer that will permit you to fulfill that promise. If your promise is related to how you will help an organization increase its revenue and reduce its costs, the logical question is, How and with what? The enabler may be a software program, service, or a suite of widgets. It could also be technology, consulting, implementation and maintenance services, financial services, and so on.

THE UNFAIR ADVANTAGE

This third component of your value proposition answers the customer question, "What makes you different from your competition?" Your unfair advantages are the capabilities, services, and offerings unique to you or your company that your competitors consider a threat to their success. An unfair advantage – such as having the largest market share, the best product, the best reputation among buyers, or the longest experience in the field – alters the playing field and gives you a distinct advantage. If you think long and hard, you will uncover several advantages you can capitalize on.

THE JUSTIFICATION

Having one or more unfair advantages is not enough. A true superstar assumes that the sell price (or initial investment) for her solution will be significantly higher that that of her competitor. She is armed with the sales tools and knowledge to specifically justify that difference. In fact, the true superstar wants her solution's initial investment to be higher than that of her competition because it speaks to value. Most customers associate quality with cost.

Let's say, for example, that you sell cars and one of your unfair advantages is that your cars have a higher trade-in value, on average, than your competition. You would want to walk your customer through the business case for investing more upfront (sell price or initial investment) than he would spend for another auto. This is called selling value!

THE PROOF

The proof is the fifth and final component of a value proposition. It provides a response to the customer statement, "I don't believe you – prove it!" The proof attests to the fact that you can do what you just said you would do. You may prove your case to the customer using industry ratings or by demonstrating market share. Without question, the very best proof comes in the form of referrals from satisfied customers, quotations in the press, or case studies showing how you improved quality or increased revenue for another account similar to your target account.

TRADE-OFFS AND THROWAWAYS

Once you determine your unfair advantage, you need to elevate it as a key buying criterion for all of your customers (see Change the Game – New Game, page 112). If it's not a key buying criterion now, you need a strategy to convince the customer that this should be a key buying criterion. For instance, let's say you are an insurance agent and your unfair advantage is the financial reputation of your company. You might say, "Mr. Customer, whether or not you buy from my company is irrelevant. As you analyze the different offerings, you need to consider the long-term viability and reputation of the companies. Are they going to be there in the future to take care of you?"

You'll notice that while elevating my unfair advantage I do not speak ill of the competition. As a superstar you should never criticize the competition. Instead, you discuss the trade-offs of the various options available to the customer. The word *trade-off* is a powerful way to positively distinguish your offering from the competition without beating them with a stick. It is a more credible way to highlight differences. You might say, "A trade-off with buying from us is that although it is typically a higher initial investment, in return you receive tremendous quality and service."

> ★ SUPERSTAR SECRET ★
>
> **Never criticize the competition. Instead, discuss the trade-offs of the various options available to the customer.**

Another way to gain credibility is by thinking about features that you can use as *throwaways,* which means to acknowledge a competitor's benefit or your product's weakness in an area that is ultimately insignificant. For example, think of a CT scanner and the number of computer cabinets it requires — otherwise known as its footprint. The footprint is not critical to the technology nor to the ultimate buying decision. Let's say your customer is looking at an Acme CT as well as yours. You might say, "Yes, I really like the small footprint of that Acme CT. You can fit a water chiller in there and it takes up very little space. Our system is a big pig compared with theirs."

You can throw that benefit away all day long. Why? You know a water chiller is not important to the customer's technological decision. The customer cares most about image quality. At this point, you can also throw in a trade-off, such as, "You know, I love those small cabinets, but that system doesn't have the spine image quality that you said was important to you."

Similarly, you can effectively highlight a competitor's benefit in a way that works for you. For instance, if one of your competitors is known in the industry for having a fantastic X-ray tube, you can be sure that rep will talk all day about her X-ray tube. Why not bring it up with the customer before she does? Why not initiate a conversation with your customer by discussing the benefits of that other tube? You could say, "You know, I have heard that Acme has an amazing tube, and I recommend that you look at them for that reason. That tube blows away the competition. I told my engineers to study it." At that point, I may use a trade-off, or I may not. I know a decision is not going to happen for eight months, after all. I must remember that my goal is to gain credibility early in the sales process. There will always be a time to highlight my own product.

In fact, given that my customers will no doubt discover my own product's weaknesses, I may choose to disclose them myself, in a manner that is less destructive, and at a time when I can gain credibility from that disclosure.

Some reps balk at the use of trade-offs and throwaways because it is so much different from the way in which they have been taught to sell, which is to talk only about your positives and never talk about your competitor. If you do talk about your competitor it will only be to beat them up. *Wrong!* This is no way to gain credibility in the eyes of your customer. This is no way to guide an account. If the customer is going to find out about a major disadvantage of my solution, do I want her to hear about it from my competitor, or do I want to tell her in the correct context? Of course I want to bring up the issue. In doing so, I gain enormous credibility with the customer. The same holds true for positive aspects of my competitor's offering. I can let the competitor highlight the positives of his solution or I can bring them up myself.

At some point, your customer will tell you, "Well, I think we are going to look at competitors X and Y." What do you say? The best answer is "Great. Those are two really good companies." You might also recommend that he look at company C, especially if it has a throwaway benefit you can highlight.

Caution: Use throwaways and trade-offs fairly sparingly, after you are certain that the benefit obtained outweighs the risk of the exposure.

If you're working for a company that has no unfair advantages, you should begin looking for another job. With no unfair advantages, you are soon going to become a commodity. The only way you will win is on price. Those are not good prospects in the long term. The message to deliver to the marketing executives in your company is that if the company does not have unfair advantages, it is in trouble. It must work hard to quickly innovate to establish unfair advantages. This is typically accomplished through technological innovation, product line expansion, mergers and acquisitions, or service enhancements.

YOUR PERSONAL VALUE PROPOSITION

In addition to your company's value proposition you need to develop your own personal value proposition, which answers the question, "Why should I buy from you in particular?" Let me give you an example by sharing my value proposition, which I customize for each customer. What is my high-level *promise?* I help drive customers' revenue and increase their profits by improving the effectiveness of their sales teams. In addition, I help participants in my sales workshops achieve critical mass sooner. Critical mass – a concept frequently mentioned by Bob Brinker on his satellite radio show, "Moneytalk" – occurs when you have earned enough to have the freedom to do what you want, when you want.

What are my *enablers?* You are reading them right now — my best practices, packaged in the form of books and customized corporate training workshops, gleaned from real-world exchanges in multiple industries. What's my *unfair advantage?* It's what makes me unique: my experience and cutting-edge content. I have more than twenty years of experience selling multimillion-dollar, high-risk, high-technology solutions and software at the CxO level for the most well-respected corporations in the world. My content is unique because it is based not on theories but on best practices that provide immediate value. My *justification* is the tremendous hard-dollar increase to both a company's top-line sales number and bottom-line net income number as a result of the immediate impact my best practices have on its sales teams. Reps will land more business at higher margins as a direct result of implementing my best practices. I can point to numerous specific, documented examples to substantiate this message. My *proof* is the millions of dollars I've earned for my employers and for myself, the recognition I've received in my profession, and my numerous customer testimonials that document the hard-dollar impact that my solutions provide.

ELEVATOR SPEECH

A shortened version of your value proposition is called your elevator speech — the spiel you might give to a potential customer who, on the elevator between floors 2 and 28, asks you, "What you do for a living?" or says, "I know you're with X company. What do you do for them?" (By the way, no matter what you're selling, nearly everyone is a potential customer. He could be in a position to buy your product or service directly, or, if you make a good impression, he could refer you to someone else who could buy your product or service. That's why it makes sense to treat every person you meet in life as if she could become your best customer.)

Some reps, caught on the elevator and asked what they do for a living, say things like, "I'm a sales rep for X company and I cover the Midwest," or "I'm a product specialist and I can help you buy a CT," or "I'm an insurance agent and I sell all types of insurance to meet your needs." These are not great responses; they do nothing to answer the underlying question, "Why should I buy from you?" They represent a missed opportunity to make an impression, establish a connection, and light a spark in a customer's mind.

A better response would be: "I help hospitals dramatically improve their profits and cut their financial recordkeeping time in half." This highlights a key pain — recordkeeping costs. Or: "I help you get where you want to go, when you want to go there — and get there safely. I own an engineering consulting firm that has repaired most of the bridges in this city." This slips in a subtle reference; although the hiring agency isn't named, *someone* hired this engineer to work on all those bridges. Or: "I help couples reduce their inheritance taxes and I give them peace of mind. I create well-thought-out estate plans." This highlights a key pain and a major benefit. Responses like these signal that you are a true consultant, a superstar. You define yourself as unique and you radiate confidence and optimism. Once you respond to the customer with your high-level promise, it is time to pause and gather more information from the customer so that you can customize the remainder of your value proposition response to their particular needs.

Many companies offer a wide range of products and services, from hardware to software to consulting services. Everyone in the company should know the value proposition for each of those lines — and for the company as a whole.

What is your company's value proposition? What is your personal value proposition? To help you think about it, below is an example of a highly customized corporate value proposition from CoverMed, an insurance company whose agents sell malpractice coverage to physician groups. If you owned a CoverMed agency,

Corporate Value Proposition

Promise	CoverMed helps physicians optimize the full clinical and financial potential of their practices by protecting both their reputations and their assets.
Enablers	CoverMed provides medical malpractice insurance and risk management educational services.
Unfair Advantages	▶ CoverMed's financial strength ensures that we will be able to pay future claims. We can withstand a tough market longer and absorb volatility better than a weaker competitor could. ▶ CoverMed's stability and longevity mean we have the best market knowledge, claims expertise, and risk management skills in the business.
Justification	Our market knowledge and claims expertise mean that your staff will spend 50% less time tracking claims. This results in a savings of approximately $10,000/year. Our financial strength means we'll be able to defend you as needed. One unprotected claim could cost you millions.
Proof	▶ Our financial strength is proven by our AM Best rating of A+ and our S&P rating of AAA. ▶ We've been in business for more than 100 years. ▶ *XYZ Report,* which tracks customer satisfaction within the insurance industry, rates CoverMed as number one. ▶ Here are several examples of customers we serve who are similar in size to your practice: _____

you would customize this corporate value proposition into a highly tailored direct message from you to your specific customer, based on that customer's specific needs. That would become your personal value proposition.

If a CoverMed sales rep found herself in an elevator with the president of a twenty-physician group medical practice known for its high physician turnover, how might she respond to the question, "What do you do for CoverMed?" I won't provide the answer; I want you to think about it. Then use **Secret Weapon 15** to develop your own value proposition.

SECRET WEAPON 15

Value Proposition Worksheet

Promise

_____
_____
_____

Enablers

_____
_____
_____

Unfair advantage(s)

_____
_____
_____

Justification

_____
_____
_____

Proof

_____
_____
_____

Elevator speech

_____
_____
_____

Once you have your company's value proposition nailed down, it's time to find some potential customers. Before you contact a potential customer, research that customer in order to thoroughly customize your value proposition.

Research Methods

Before I approach a prospective customer I first thoroughly research the company and the CxO. I research the person using online search engines such as Google.com, Yahoo.com, and Ask.com to find out if he or she has been quoted anywhere, has participated in industry groups, or has been in the news for any reason. I try to get a feel for the CxO's personality, background, and interests before I'm introduced.

To research the target company I consult online resources such as Hoover's, Inc. (www.hoovers.com), OneSource Information Services, Inc. (www.onesource.com), and Edgar Online, Inc. (www.edgar-online.com), all available by subscription. In addition, I review several years' worth of the company's annual reports, often available on the target's Web site. If not, I call the company and request them. Then and only then am I ready to move to the next step, turning on the Prospecting Machine.

Prospecting Machine™

You can't buy a Prospecting Machine at Sam's Club or Costco. You can't even find one online. What you can do, however, is set up a high-quality, easily replicated, thoroughly documented process – a machine that, once you set it up and keep cranking the handle, chugs along nicely and regularly spits out well-qualified prospects. Here is the parts list for assembling your machine:

- ▸ Your company's value proposition, customized as appropriate
- ▸ Database management software (e.g., Microsoft Excel)
- ▸ Word-processing software (e.g., Microsoft Word, WordPerfect)
- ▸ Calendar/contacts software (e.g., Microsoft Outlook, ACT!)
- ▸ Power Letter (**Secret Weapon 16**)
- ▸ Power Phone Script (**Secret Weapon 17**)
- ▸ Territory Attack Plan (**Secret Weapon 18**)

Once you have the machine assembled, you pour into it a high-quality list of contacts based on your target market (researched through OneSource, Hoover's, Edgar Online, etc.) and season the mix with your organizational skills, drive, persistence, dedication, and confidence. Out come high-quality leads.

Prospecting Machine

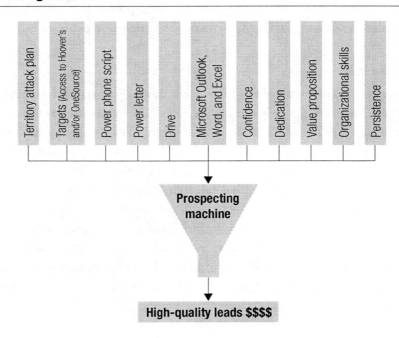

If you follow a routine, prospecting quickly becomes painless and second nature. The goal of the routine is to find prospects who have: (1) business headaches that your product or solution can eliminate, and (2) the desire to eliminate them. Here's how you find the prospects:

- Find a database of target customers.
- Set up an Excel contacts database.
- In Excel, enter the names, titles, and addresses of prospective customers from your research sources.
- For each prospect, contact the CxO's executive assistant for confirmation of the CxO's name (make sure you find out the exact spelling and how he or she prefers to be addressed), the CxO's mailing address, e-mail address, and direct line, if possible.
- Create a mail-merge-ready Power Letter template (Secret Weapon 16) in Word.
- Mail-merge the Excel contacts database with the Power Letter template.
- Adapt and customize the individual letters as needed. Proof each one carefully!
- Print out the Power Letters on your letterhead.

- ▸ Create an envelope template in Word.

- ▸ Address the letters and apply postage (you may wish to use an online postal services site such as www.stamps.com).

- ▸ Mail-merge the Excel contacts database with the envelope template.

- ▸ Print out the envelopes. Stuff and mail. Don't forget to include your business card.

- ▸ Export the Excel contacts database to Outlook.

- ▸ Set up one-week follow-up reminders for each contact in Outlook.

- ▸ Write your Power Phone Script (Secret Weapon 17).

- ▸ One week after you mail the Power Letters, make follow-up calls using your Power Phone Script.

- ▸ Schedule appointments.

- ▸ Spend your huge commissions on something extravagant!

Power Letter

A power letter – **Secret Weapon 16** – is one effective tool for gaining access to senior levels of an account. Of course, it is not the only way to gain access to senior management. Your first choice would be a referral. Perhaps someone at a lower level of an existing account or maybe a senior executive at account A would be willing to contact his buddy at account B on your behalf. Referrals are nice to have, but hard to come by, so we'll discuss the specifics of how to construct and deploy a power letter.

At the top of the letter you insert an attention-getting quote that relates specifically to your target – for example, "ABC Corporation has recognized $100 million in savings in the last 12 months using Adams & Associates' solutions. – Lee Gannon, SVP, ABC Corporation." The purpose of the quote is to highlight a specific business objective – in this case, the desire to decrease expenses. You could also use a quote from a recognized industry expert saying something favorable about your company or describing an industry-wide problem that your company remedies. If you can find a quote that is on topic from the CEO or board member of your target account, often times that is the very best quote.

In the body of the letter, use phrases that show you have done your homework, that highlight a key customer pain, and that prove you have solved the same problem for others – in other words, a reference. It's very important to use the word *opinion* in the close. People may not want to chat with a sales rep, but they *love* sharing their opinions. Use an assumptive close in the letter (consultative closing techniques will be discussed in Gaining Commitment, page 143). Tell the

SECRET WEAPON 16

Power Letter

Use an attention-getting quote that relates specifically to your target.

 **Adams** & Associates

"ABC Corporation has recognized $100 million in savings in the last 12 months using Adams & Associates' solutions." —Lee Gannon, SVP, ABC Corporation

Ms. Maria Isner
Chief Financial Officer
SISU Corporation
4143 Pine Street
San Francisco, CA 94104

Dear Maria:

Show that you have done your homework.

Highlight a key customer pain.

After a two-week review of your financials, I have noticed that the increase in your costs in the last quarter has outpaced the growth of your revenue.

Show that you have solved the same problem for others.

Adams & Associates has helped numerous business partners turn around their performance. The results quoted at the top of this letter are common. Leading enterprise customers such as Dell, Motorola, Exxon Mobil, Cisco, and 50 of the Fortune 100 have used our solutions to automate all aspects of procurement, significantly reducing costs and **therefore increasing shareholder value.**

Specifically, our customers are enjoying the following benefits:

▶ 30% cycle time reduction, allowing a quicker reaction to changes in their business

▶ 64% decrease in errors, thanks to automated order entry

▶ 52% reduction of effort by procurement staff, increasing the capacity of their team

I look forward to meeting with you to get your opinion on how Adams & Associates may be able to help SISU Corporation realize similar or even greater results before the end of this calendar year.

Request the recipient's opinion.

Sincerely,

Ben

Benjamin Edwards
cell 630-555-1212

Put the time and date of your planned phone call in a postscript, because postscripts are the first thing most people read.

P.S. I will call your office on Tuesday, October 19, at 9:00 a.m. If this time is inconvenient, please have Laura contact me to reschedule.

Refer to the recipient's executive assistant, which shows once again that you've done your homework.

recipient that you will be contacting his or her "office" (in the generic version of the letter) or his or her "executive assistant" (in a customized letter) to set up a meeting. Be sure to mention the executive assistant's name. Put this last bit of information in a postscript, where it is sure to be read.

When you're sending out power letters, quality is much more important than quantity. Rather than sending five hundred letters per week, send only ten or twelve. This gives you the time you need to customize each letter and ensures that you will be able to follow up. Be careful about thoroughly customizing the letter to the recipient. The last thing you want to mail out is a letter addressed to "Ms. Schwartz" that refers to some other person (worst of all, Ms. Schwartz's competitor) somewhere else in the letter. Be scrupulous in your proofreading. Better yet, have a colleague proofread every letter before it's mailed.

The number of accounts for which you are responsible will obviously dictate the level of effort you can put into each letter. If you are responsible for half the United States and you are planning a mass mailing, you'll need to use a generic letter.

Power Phone Script

The principles behind the power letter and power phone script are the same. The purpose of both is to establish credibility and build trust – to climb the left side of the Trust Triangle. When you call the prospective customer to follow up, you cover much the same points you made in the power letter, depending on the call. Depending on the industry, skipping the letter and starting with a phone call may or may not work. When I was selling multimillion-dollar solutions to the CxOs of major corporations, I found I couldn't get through by phone; there were too many gatekeepers. With lower-level executives, starting with a phone call may be best. The bottom line is, do whatever works. Experiment. Then lock in a process that fits your solution and target market.

There is no one right way to have a phone conversation; you should speak naturally. Thinking in advance, however, about what you might say will help the conversation flow more smoothly. Rehearse the phrases in **Secret Weapon 17** in front of a mirror. Your anxiety will decrease as you get used to feeling them roll off your tongue. The last thing you want to do is to sound like you're parroting a script. Very few people can deliver an excellent customized power script without notes, so keep them close at hand, but do your best to sound natural. Pay attention to what the customer is actually saying, and respond accordingly. Relax. You're in a position to provide valuable assistance to this customer; allow yourself to feel confident and self-assured.

SECRET WEAPON 17

Power Phone Script

Statement	Comments
"I have spent several days researching your financial statements."	*This positions you as someone who does his or her homework.*
"I see that the increase in your costs in the last quarter has outpaced the growth in your revenue."	*Touch on a key customer pain.*
"We've had very good luck helping others facing the same challenges. Not just company X, which I mentioned in my letter — we've also helped companies Y and Z."	*Shows that you have solved the same problem for others. References build credibility and are the most powerful way to get your foot in the door for a meeting.*
"I'm following up as I promised I would in my letter."	*This establishes you as a person who keeps his or her promises.*
"Is this a good time to talk?"	*Superstars are always respectful of the customer's time. If now is not a good time, ask the customer when you may call back.*
"Didn't you serve on the X quality control panel last year?"	*This shows that you've taken the time to know your customer — but not to the extent that the customer feels like he or she is being intruded on. Do not volunteer the fact that you Googled the customer.*
"I read your comments in X magazine about the new safety measures in Congress. That was a thoughtful analysis."	*If you can offer a compliment with sincerity, do so. If you cannot, do not. Do not make things up; even customers who like flattery can sniff out phoniness.*
"I'd like to get your opinion on how we might be of help to you."	*Request the customer's opinion. "Opinion" is a power word. Even people who hate talking to sales reps love to share their opinions.*
"I'm in the business of helping my customers prevent headaches."	*Position yourself as a consultative rep as opposed to a peddler of products or services.*
"We've found that the sooner a company adopts our solution, the more quickly they start saving money. Y company boosted their revenue by X percent within six months."	*Mention the bottom-line benefit of your solution.*
"I'll be in your area next Wednesday and Thursday. Would either day work for you?"	*Use an Alternate Choice Close (page 144) to ask for a face-to-face meeting.*
"Is there anything else you'd like me to know before our meeting?"	*This gives the customer the opportunity to begin relying on you right this moment as a consultant.*
"I look forward to meeting with you."	*Talk to customers with the degree of politeness you would employ if you were speaking with the Queen of England.*

The following phone tips are worth reviewing:

- Your theme during the call should be consistent: You have done your homework and you believe that you understand the customer's pain. "We have had a tremendous amount of success addressing a very similar pain with another well-respected company in your industry. I'd like to meet with you to see if we may be able to assist you. When would be a good time for us to meet?"

- Don't take hard positions. Avoid statements such as: "You will save X…," "We never…," "You will receive…," "We always…," or "You have to…."

- Use softer, more believable statements such as: "I believe you will find…," "I'm confident that…," "You may discover…," "You might…," and "You could…."

- Use the power word: *opinion*. As in, "I'd like to get your opinion on how we have assisted others and how that experience might be applicable to your situation."

- Never interrupt the customer. Let the customer completely finish what she is saying.

- Ask clarifying questions to make sure you understand what the customer is saying.

- Be respectful without kowtowing.

- Remember that this conversation is not about you! It's about your customer and his current and specific challenges.

- No whining – about anything. No complaints about the weather, your bursitis, or the dead batteries in your cell phone. Choose to be upbeat. People are attracted to upbeat people and repelled by complainers.

- Choose a friendly, confident (but not cocky) tone.

- Use impeccable manners.

The key to success with the Prospecting Machine is dedication. Dedicate a time to turn on the machine once or twice a week and you will be pleased with the results. Your goal is not to sell the customer with either the letter or the phone call but rather to get your toe in the door for a face-to-face meeting.

Territory Attack Plan

While you're handling the selling process at the micro (individual customer) level, your company is also looking at it from the macro (company-wide) level.

SECRET WEAPON 18

Territory Attack Plan

Date: April 1, 2008

Executive Summary
- Background
- Strategy and Fiscal Year 2009 Goals

2009

Territory Map
- Strategic Territory Management
  - Strategic Vendor Concept
  - Territory Philosophy—Strategic Selling Road Map
- General Territory Description
- Current Business Climate
  - Industries Represented
  - Market Size
  - Systems Presence
  - Competition
  - Consulting Firm Presence
  - Prospect Details

Territory Mission, Strategy, and Goals
- Overall Territory Mission
- Strategy
- Fiscal Year 2009 Goals

Tactical Approach
- General Tactics
- Tactical Guidelines
- General Messages

> In this territory attack plan, the superstar rep and managers set sales goals for the coming year and measure progress to date in the current year.

2008

Fiscal Year 2008 Progress to Date
- Revenue Forecast Highlights
  - Current Revenue Forecast
  - Delta from 2008 Revenue Forecast of 12-31-2007
- Wins/Losses
  - Wins
  - Losses
- 2008 Targets
  - Best Candidates for Fiscal Year 2008 Business
  - Reasonable Chance for Fiscal Year 2008
  - Fair Chance for Fiscal Year 2008
  - Others in the Pipeline
- Account Activity Highlights
  - Cornerstone Accounts
  - Account Activities
- Forecast Resource Requirements for Q-1
  - January Resources
  - February Resources
  - March Resources

- Estimated Resource Requirements for Q-2
- Estimated Resource Requirements for Q-3
- Estimated Resource Requirements for Q-4
- Partnership Highlights
  - Tier 1 Partners
  - Tier 2 Partners

Key Challenges Limiting Success
- Corporate Visit Coordination
- Management Communication
- OEM Strategy

Territory Account Progress Summary

Territory Partner Progress Summary

Account Business Review Sheets

Sales reps usually create a territory attack plan in consultation with their sales manager. The plan is an in-house map for approaching your territory. Superstars have a responsibility to provide accurate forecasts for their company. Having command of your accounts allows you to truly commit to your manager when you promise a sale. This, in turn, makes your manager's job easier and facilitates the accurate forecasting that your company requires. Taking the time to put together a powerful plan – and reviewing it periodically – will help you prioritize where to spend your time and energy and help you stay focused.

Secret Weapon 18 displays the table of contents from a superstar's territory attack plan. An actual plan could run twenty-five pages or more, depending on the product or service and the sophistication of the sales division. In this example, dated April 1, 2008, the sales division is assessing the current business climate, reviewing its sales strategy, planning ahead for the next fiscal year, reporting on progress so far in the current fiscal year, and comparing current performance with earlier projections. The sales team is also assessing the current targets and making sure they have the necessary resources for approaching those targets.

> ★ **SUPERSTAR SECRET** ★
>
> **The conversation is not about you! It's about the customer's needs.**

The point of the territory attack plan is not to create endless paperwork; the point is to think ahead, always assessing whether where you're putting your energy is a direction in which you're likely to succeed. Such complex, long-term forecasting efforts – and indeed, most of the techniques and concepts outlined in this book – are appropriate mostly for products and services with long sales cycles.

Your territory attack plan will look different, but I include the one in Secret Weapon 18 to give you an idea of the highly detailed, thoughtful planning necessary for success.

So you have researched your list of prospects, developed your value proposition, and turned on your Prospecting Machine. With an eye on your company's territory attack plan, you finally have some potential customers to contact. Now what?

▶ Step 2 — Qualifying Prospects ◀

True or false: You should work every opportunity presented to you, and you should work every opportunity equally. Early in my career, I spent time selling to everybody. Later in my career I learned how to qualify prospects very, very quickly.

In the Basics of Selling, we were all taught to work as hard as we can to get every opportunity, and make sure every opportunity comes to the table. A superstar sees things differently. She thinks carefully about the proper utilization of resources, both personal and corporate, because she knows those resources are both valuable and scarce. For some sales reps it is enlightening to realize the cost of sales for their company. Not just the company car and your expenses but marketing and support staff payroll can represent 8% to 10% of the total amount of the sale. Think about this as you decide whether to deploy resources on an account. Be sure you are chasing good business.

Also consider your personal cost of sales. Imagine yourself working for months on an account — hosting site visits, bringing in specialists, and so forth — only to find out that the customer doesn't have the budget for the purchase or that the customer has involved a consultant that you didn't know about. You very well know the toll this takes on your personal life.

I put the value of the time I spend with a customer at $10,000 per minute. Perhaps that sounds arrogant. The way I see it, however, when customers meet with me they are getting the benefit of expertise that has taken me twenty-five years to develop. So you can bet that I am going to meet with a customer only if I think we have a mutual long-term interest in moving forward. I don't meet with customers who don't respect my time or who won't help me find the answers to basic questions.

> ★ SUPERSTAR SECRET ★
>
> **Don't waste scarce resources on dead-end prospects. Qualify quickly!**

You, too, cannot afford to spin your wheels with customers. Your time is too valuable to be meeting with customers who aren't ready to move forward or aren't willing to assist you. It is your responsibility to use your company's valuable resources wisely. You can't waste precious assets, such as the expenses related to presentations and demonstrations, the technical support staff's time, and your manager's time. You have limited time and energy to devote to your workday. It would be a tragedy for you to chase after business for months, only to find out that you lost because you did not properly qualify the opportunity. So qualify quickly! Don't waste scarce resources on dead-end prospects. If this happens repeatedly, "special assignment" is waiting for you.

Learning from Your Losses

One prospect wasted twelve months of my time because the company didn't have the budget for the purchase. In another deal I lost to Philips, one of GE's biggest competitors, not even knowing that Philips was competing for the business. Another time, while working for Cisco Systems, I experienced a very painful loss that showed me the value of understanding who the decision maker is and the importance of selling high in the organization. It was a classic situation in which I sold to the midlevel, assuming the midlevel was the decision maker, only to find out that the CFO was in charge. At the end of the negotiations, the midlevel manager at the hospital left me a voice mail saying, "Congratulations, Dan — we're going with Cisco!" I forwarded the message to my manager and crowed to everyone about winning the multimillion-dollar deal. A week later the midlevel hospital manager called back and said, "Sorry, Dan. We changed our minds. We're going with one of your competitors."

Why did the customer choose the competition? I was outsold. I would have prevented this loss if I had properly qualified this opportunity. Much to my unhappy surprise, my competitor used strategy called Change the Game — Expand the Pie, one of the eight major account strategies. (The others, which will be discussed in the Strategy section beginning on page 106, are Sole Source; Frontal Attack; Change the Game — Reduce the Pie; Change the Game — New Game; Accelerate; Delay; and Disengage.) With Expand the Pie the rep says, in effect, "Mr. or Ms. Customer, rather than looking at just product A, you should really be considering products A, B, C, and D — and I think that when you consider all of those, you'll want to give us the business for A+B+C+D." Although in a head-to-head comparison of our product A to the competitor's product A, we were the clear winner, we couldn't compete with their A+B+C+D offering. Plus, the competitor used a Change the Game — New Game strategy by changing who was involved in the decision process. They were selling higher up in the organization — above my head to the CFO. So I was outflanked on two fronts. I learned a lot from that loss. One key takeaway is that being wary can be beneficial. The deal is never done, and you must get to the person who's signing the check!

This loss was particularly painful because of all the resources that I, in hindsight, had wasted on the sale. I had been in conversation with the customer for more than a year, pulling in the engineers from my organization to assist me in the sale. I provided a tremendous amount of value to the hospital. I forecasted the deal, I won the deal… but I didn't push it over the finish line.

Recovering psychologically from a loss like that can be challenging. You learn to develop a healthy paranoia — a keen awareness at all times of what's going on around you. When you lose a sale, it helps to be part of an organization whose culture responds to losses gracefully. I was lucky. My manager would say, "Well, you lost that one, but there's always tomorrow. You're a great rep — you know your stuff." I would internally say to myself, "I was outsold. That is unacceptable, and it won't happen again."

My losses were actually helpful, because they taught me how to prevent future pain for myself, for my workshop participants, and for you. In response to my pain, I developed the BMPCC tool **(Secret Weapon 19)**.

Be My Perfect Cash Cow (BMPCC)

When you're trying to qualify an opportunity, you need to ask five key questions.

- ▸ What is the customer's **Budget?**
- ▸ Who is the key decision **Maker?**
- ▸ Where is the customer in his buying **Process?**
- ▸ Who is the **Competition?**
- ▸ What are the customer's decision-making **Criteria?**

An easy way to remember these questions is with the acronym BMPCC – "Be My Perfect Cash Cow." You will lose deals if you don't know the answers to these questions early enough in the buying process. Plus, if you discover the answers late rather than early, there's no way to devise a strategy to compensate. (The BMPCC template will show up again later, when you're ready to formulate your strategic plan.)

SECRET WEAPON 19

BMPCC Account Qualification Template

B	What is the customer's **Budget**?	$
M	Who is the key decision **Maker**?	
P	What is the customer's buying **Process**?	
	Compelling event: What?	
	Compelling event: When?	
C	Who are our **Competitors**?	
	What are they offering?	
	What is their strategy?	
C	What are the customer's decision-making **Criteria** (rack and stack)?	

A superstar needs to know the *B* in BMPCC: What is the budget? Does the customer have the financial ability to close and the willingness to move forward?

And a superstar needs to know the *M,* the decision maker or makers. How many are there? What are their previous experiences in purchases such as this? What are their personality profiles? I don't want to be involved with a customer for months and then lose the deal because I didn't know who the decision maker was. This seems so simple, but I lost business early on for just that reason. I spent hours working with a customer, walking him down what seemed like a mutually agreed upon pathway, only to find out that the decision maker wasn't the middle manager, the guy I had been working with. It was the CFO. And I lost the deal.

In BMPCC, the *P* stands for process – the importance of which was stressed during the discussion of D^3 in chapter 3. It is imperative that you uncover this early on. Remember, we're not talking about the sales process here. Our focus is on the customer's buying process – and specifically, the customer's compelling event (also discussed in chapter 3).

The first *C* in BMPCC stands for competitors. You need to know what other vendors the customer is considering, along with the strengths and weaknesses of their offerings. Sometimes you are not competing against a vendor at all. Your competition may be your customer's inactivity – she may decide to maintain the status quo and do nothing, or she may allocate her budget dollars to a different project altogether.

The last *C* stands for decision criteria: As the customer begins looking at various solutions, on what will she base her decision? Frequently the customer's initial key decision criteria fall into the following categories:

- ▸ Initial selling price
- ▸ Service and support
- ▸ Performance
- ▸ Upgradeability
- ▸ Risk/reputation

Once the customer lists the decision criteria, you then need to know their priority and ranking, otherwise known as the rack and stack. Which criterion is most important to the customer? Price? Performance? Or speed of installation?

Once you know those criteria, you can either deliver a solution that matches them (assuming you have one), or you can Change the Game (discussed later in this chapter) – that is, try to influence the customer's assessment of which criterion is most important. For instance, if the customer says that price is his number one priority, and your offering is not the lower-priced one, your job would be to reframe his evaluation of the various offerings to focus more on, say, performance or ROI. If you're unable to reframe his evaluation criteria, at least you know ahead of time — and not eight months down the road — that you have a problem.

During one sale for GE I uncovered a buying criterion that surprised me. I was selling to a hospital with a new CEO. I had been selling to this hospital for years and had cultivated friendly relationships with other officers of the hospital, but had difficulty getting access to the new CEO. I finally managed to arrange a sit-down meeting with him (using Secret Weapon 16 — Power Letter), albeit with considerable reluctance on his part. As soon as we began talking, he blasted my company for a bad experience he had had five years earlier with a faulty GE home refrigerator. Talk about holding a grudge! I grabbed the stick from the CEO's hand, so to speak, and beat up myself and GE for the faulty fridge. "This is unacceptable," I said. "I can understand why you are upset. This is not the level of service you can expect from us, and I apologize." With the information he gave me, plus some internal research, I solved his refrigerator problem to his satisfaction.

Now that I understood that post-sales support was the CEO's number one buying criterion, I quickly changed our campaign to focus on our superior service department. I related this high-quality service and support to the equipment I was trying to sell him, and eventually won a $2.1 million order from him for his hospital.

Traditional selling theories that encourage "the customer is always right" mindset allow the customer to reprimand the rep for commitments not met. They teach reps to exercise account control by "accepting the stick" — to sit there and take it. A true consultant beats *himself* up in front of the customer when things go wrong. Can you see how this helps you climb the left side of the triangle?

You have to be careful not to qualify too soon, or your customer may get upset with you. Customers don't want to sit back while you nail your five Be My Perfect Cash Cow questions. As we discussed earlier, the conversation should be about them, not about you. On the other hand, you don't wait six months, either. Try to get your answers in the first couple of calls.

> ★ SUPERSTAR SECRET ★
>
> **The number one credibility tool is a blank sheet of paper.**

If I said to a customer, "I could provide more value to you if you could share with me what your buying process will be. What is your evaluation process for this major purchase?" And the customer said to me, "Sorry, I'll never share that with you," then I would know right away that I was not in control of that buying process and I was not going to win. Therefore, I would reconsider my current sales strategy and find a way go above or around him in the organization — and if I was unsuccessful, perhaps adopt a Disengage strategy and bow out altogether.

COW Questioning Technique

True or false: The main reason sales reps ask questions is to uncover needs. False. Superstars realize that questioning goes way beyond this. Insightful, finely tuned questions can establish your credibility and earn the customer's trust. The number one credibility tool for a superstar is a blank sheet of paper onto which you make notes about the customer's conversation. The goal is to listen to the customer instead of launching into reasons why the customer should buy. Great questioning – which provides key information needed to qualify, set strategy, and gain credibility – requires research and preparation.

Questions can also kill – if they're the wrong ones or at the wrong time. Asking too many questions, or asking questions that reveal you have not researched the company, can decrease your credibility. Only ask questions that reveal you have done your homework and you know something about the customer's business. The questions I ask customers fall into three categories and add up to COW:

- ▸ **C** – questions about their *current* situation (e.g., "What do you like about your current situation? What do you dislike?")

- ▸ **O** – questions about their *optimal* situation (e.g., "In a perfect world, if you could design your own solution for your needs and challenges with unlimited funds, what would that solution look like?")

- ▸ **W** – questions about the *win* that the proposed solution would provide for the corporation (e.g., "How does your company or department win if the optimal state is realized?") or for the individual customer (e.g., "Assuming that these needs and challenges are solved, how would your department or company benefit [win]? How would this affect you personally?")

These personal impact questions are the most powerful; they provide valuable insights about the customer that can be continually referenced and leveraged throughout the sales process.

Power Quid Pro Quo Letter

Sometimes customers hesitate when it comes to providing the information you've asked for during the qualification process, but they may be willing to trade – that is, do a quid pro quo. A caution, however: Never state this transaction quite so baldly, or you'll offend your customer. In most cases, the customer should never *feel* like you're using a quid pro quo response; he should feel as though the two of you are just cooperating and swapping reasonable business favors. Round the corners on what you say so that the customer does not feel manipulated.

Secret Weapon 20 shows a letter from superstar Ben to his prospective customer, Lee, that summarizes their understanding. Ben has agreed to pick up the expenses of Lee and a colleague when they travel to evaluate Ben's proposed solution. In exchange, Lee has promised to provide access by Ben to the senior-level executives in Lee's company, so that Ben can explore other ways to be of assistance. You may notice that Secret Weapon 20 is what could be called a roaring quid pro quo letter, because the corners are not rounded. It is a very sharp example of quid pro quo. Typically, this is not recommended. In this case, however, the customer had a history of failing to carry through on commitments, so the harshness was necessary. Another instance in which a roaring quid pro quo is appropriate is a crunch time – when the customer is demanding that you lower price. Superstars know that a drop in price is considered only in exchange for one thing… the order.

Here's another example of the use of quid pro quo, one used later on in the sales process. Pete, the customer, says, "I need you to move up your delivery date by six weeks." Your response could be, "Pete, you know that I am always happy to do what I can to help you out. I have scarce resources to deploy, but I'd be happy to do what I can for you. Maybe you could help me. You know how we talked about the benefits of approving the service agreement at the time of the equipment purchase? Is there any chance you could help me out in getting that pushed through your internal processes?"

Responding to Surprise Proposal Requests

When I was a new rep I remember approaching my manager to report, "A prospect just called out of the blue, and she wants us to give her a formal presentation tomorrow!" I jumped to fulfill the customer's request, thinking that I had to sing to the customer's tune. Has that happened to you?

The fact that the request comes as a surprise is not good. It means you had no prior knowledge that the customer is about to buy a big product or solution. If you are covering your territory properly, this should not happen. You should know far in advance. If you're surprised by the request, then all of the following are probably true:

- ▸ You have not established trust with the customer.
- ▸ The customer did not want you involved early in this process.
- ▸ You did not help the customer put together the request for proposal.
- ▸ Your competitor probably helped your customer with the proposal request.
- ▸ The decision is soon.

SECRET WEAPON 20

Power Quid Pro Quo Letter

Lee Gannon
Senior Vice President
ABC Corporation
18 Thorndike Road
Wakefield, MA 01880

Dear Lee:

Thank you for considering Adams & Associates' equipment for your new Imaging System project. This note confirms our discussion today regarding the plan for your evaluation of our solutions.

Adams & Associates agrees to cover all the costs involved in ABC Corporation's evaluation of our equipment. These costs include airfare, ground transportation, meals, and hotel accommodations for two decision makers. The estimated total cost is approximately $18,575.

In return, ABC Corporation has agreed to the following:

▶ Adams & Associates will be given the opportunity to provide a comprehensive formal presentation of our equipment solution to all decision makers.

▶ Prior to the presentation and site visit, Adams & Associates will consult with key parties so we can thoroughly understand their decision criteria, specific needs, and decision process.

▶ Adams & Associates will be given the opportunity, if deemed appropriate by Adams & Associates, to meet with your senior-level executives (CFO, CMO, COO) to review how Adams & Associates may be able to assist ABC Corporation beyond simply providing equipment.

I look forward to assisting you with this exciting new Imaging System project.

Sincerely,

Ben

Benjamin Edwards
cell 630-555-1212

cc: Alice Murphy, MD

- You are behind the eight-ball.
- You have no answers to the BMPCC questions.
- You have no strategy.
- You are beginning a Frontal Attack (described later – not good!).

Given those factors, you will *not* win this deal. But early on, I didn't know that. Like most reps, when these surprise requests came in I would roll up my sleeves, call in my specialists, cancel my weekend plans, and compile a gigantic formal response. I made this mistake several times, before I learned there is a much better way. After all, you have not been working with this customer; you don't even know for sure whether she is in the market for your product – you haven't qualified her yet. You don't refuse the request; in fact, you always say, "Sure, I can do that." But then you convince the customer that you could better serve her interests another way.

You might say, "I can certainly do a formal presentation tomorrow, but honestly, I don't think it would be in your best interests. I can talk all day, but unless I know where your primary concerns are, I will waste your time. I don't want to do that. What if we sit down and review your specific challenges, needs, and requirements?" By doing so you are selecting two strategies and laying the groundwork for a possible third. By trying to change the customer's buying process you are employing Change the Game – New Game. By trying to get the customer to put off the decision, you are also using the Delay strategy as a secondary strategy. Finally, if the customer does not agree to your request to meet the key decision makers, you may consider a Disengage strategy.

Secret Weapon 21, Response to a Surprise Proposal Request, is a carefully worded letter to the prospect. Like all the secret weapons shared here, feel free to adapt it to your needs. This secret weapon is also a great example of quid pro quo: "I'll respond if you delay and allow us access to your key decision makers."

There are risks inherent in responding this way. You may argue yourself out of the opportunity altogether. On the other hand, you were not even in the game to begin with, and your resources and those of your company are limited.

▶ Step 3 — Selecting the Strategy ◀

Strategy is my favorite area of sales. This is where the magic happens, and where your enthusiasm and intellect are rewarded. There are several books and programs on the topic of sales strategy, but most are either highly theoretical or extremely paperwork-intensive. I have yet to see a program that is worth the time required by the rep to populate all the data requested. For the superstar, all these programs do

SECRET WEAPON 21

Response to a Surprise Proposal Request

Lindsay Johnson
Senior Vice President
Baker Corporation
32434 State Street
Montpelier, VT 05602

Dear Lindsay:

Thank you for inviting us to provide a proposal for your new system. We appreciate your confidence in us.

Adams & Associates' policy is to not respond to requests for proposals (or bids) until we have had an opportunity to interview the heads of the department or departments that will be affected by the scope of the project. We have found that this policy enables us to provide value for our customers and results in a more satisfactory implementation. You, as the customer, are the main beneficiary.

If you would help arrange a meeting for us with the VP of Operations and the CFO, we would be happy to invest the time and resources necessary to fully respond to your request for proposal. I would be happy to get together at your convenience.

Thank you for this opportunity to grow the long-term relationship between Adams & Associates and Baker Corporation.

Sincerely,

Ben

Benjamin Edwards
cell 630-555-1212

is create busy work and kill trees. I dare to claim that the eight major account strategies outlined later in this chapter will serve you better than any other sales strategy program on the market – and will save a few trees!

Choosing the right strategy at the right time requires an appreciation of the complexity of the decision process, both from the customer's perspective and that of your company. Typically, the larger the company, the more complicated things get. Complex decisions require a superstar's strategic expertise, because these decisions are not static, but ever-changing; a superstar adjusts her sales approach accordingly. A strategy is selected based on how well it positions you to win the deal and crush your competition. You select the one that will maximize your offering in the customer's mind relative to those of your competitors.

> ★ SUPERSTAR SECRET ★
>
> **Don't let the customer define the path ahead. Define it yourself with this philosophy: My field! My time! My game! My rules!**

The strategy you select serves as a compass that not only guides you in the right direction – it creates the path. If you are team-selling, then it helps the team know which way to paddle the boat, so that you are all working toward a common goal. Don't let the customer define the path ahead; define it yourself with this philosophy: My field! My time! My game! My rules!

Picture a Roman coliseum. The spectators in the stands are all your customers. In the middle of the coliseum you and your top three competitors are hacking at each other with swords and cudgels. The customers are witnessing the battle with great enjoyment – there's nothing more entertaining than watching the four of you go at it. Many reps fall into this trap, because they don't know any better. After all, the customer sets it up by ordering everyone into the ring.

I don't play that game. Only on rare occasions do you need to play the role of the gladiator. The only time you will put on your gladiator gear is when your current offering is seen in the customer's mind (not in your marketing department's mind) as being ten times better than that of your closest competitor (see Frontal Attack, page 110). This *may* happen when you announce a new breakthrough product. The reason I say "may" is that although you may have a cool new product with lots of sizzle, you may discover that the customer doesn't care about sizzle. In fact, he doesn't even like sizzle. He's the king of anti-sizzle. And you'll get slaughtered in the ring. Usually there is a much better way.

So you're sitting in your manager's office. She asks, "What is your strategy for winning this opportunity?" An average rep might say, "I'm taking the customer on a site visit," or "I'm going to have my specialist give them a presentation," or "I'm going to offer them a really great price." A superstar would research the customer, put together a strategic plan, select one of the eight major account strategies, and back it up with sound tactics in order to carry out the mission of trouncing the competition. He would be able to articulate why he chose that particular strategy and outline the tactics to support the plan.

Anatomy of a Strategic Plan

You put together a strategic plan by asking yourself a series of questions. As you find the answers, you summarize them on **Secret Weapon 22** – Strategic Plan. Strategy is not fixed; it may change based on changes in the customer or competitive environment. Keep the strategic plan updated as you go along. That way you'll always have an at-a-glance assessment of where you are in your selling process, where the customer is in her buying process, and what you need to do next. For instance, if the plan shows that you are still on the left side of the Trust Triangle, you know that it is emphatically *not* the right time to dump data on the customer or ask for the sale. Instead, it's time to continue developing trust using all the techniques we discussed earlier. Let's look at the components of a strategic plan.

- ▶ *Account Overview.* An account overview is a summary of the account history, the current situation in the account, and the CEO's key initiatives. In the account overview you also might note, from your research, the profitability challenges the customer is facing, or the political issues under debate by its board of directors, or an indication as to whether this entity prefers to lease rather than buy outright. What are the customer's targeted growth areas? Its weakest divisions? Its current installed base? A sales manager will expect a superstar sales rep to know these things.

- ▶ *Opportunity.* Next the superstar defines the nature of the opportunity, both short and long term. What product or solution is being offered? What is the target sale amount?

- ▶ *Decision Process.* Earlier we explained that the superstar sales process marries the customer's (informal) decision process with the (formal) customer buying process. Knowing one is not acceptable – you must know both. Where is the key decision maker(s) on the Trust Triangle?

- ▶ *Buying Process.* The superstar then describes the buying process the customer will be following. What is the compelling event? One of the steps in the customer buying process will be to finalize vendor selection. You need to know when the customer plans to do this. Who are your competitors, and what are they offering? A superstar rep needs to

SECRET WEAPON 22

Strategic Plan

Account Overview	
Research findings	
CxO's top 3 goals	
Biggest challenges	
Customer's #1 competitor	
Customer's #1 customer	
Top 3 industry trends	

Opportunity	
Product/solution	
Target sale amount	
Expected order date	

Decision Process	
Where is the key decision maker? (Mark estimated spot on the Trust Triangle.)	The Trust Triangle

Buying Process		
B	What is the customer's **Budget**?	
M	Who is the key decision **Maker**?	
P	What are the steps in the customer's buying **Process**?	
	Compelling event: What?	
	Compelling event: When?	
C	Who are our **Competitors**?	
	What are they offering?	
	What is their strategy?	
C	What are the customer's decision-making **Criteria** (rack and stack)?	

Key Players	
Who is our main customer contact?	
Who else is involved?	
Are we selling at the CxO level?	
What are the key customer objections?	
How are we selling value?	

Solution Differentiation	
Based on the customer's decision-making criteria, exactly how do we plan to differentiate our offering?	
Do we have a platinum bullet?	

SECRET WEAPON 22 (continued)

Strategic Plan

Strategy	
Which of the 8? 1) Sole source; 2) Frontal attack; 3) Expand the pie; 4) Reduce the pie; 5) New game; 6) Accelerate; 7) Delay; 8) Disengage	
Why this strategy now?	
Tactics	
Completion date	
Tactic 1	
Tactic 2	
Tactic 3	

know all about the competition. I'm not talking about just their names and their products — you need to know their experience, their approach, even the cars they drive. (Pay attention! If you see their cars in the customer parking lot or their names in sign-in books, you know they're selling against you!) What are their selling styles? Which of the eight major account strategies are they deploying? You should know what the competition is doing at all times. Much of this comes with experience. You can also find out what the competition is up to by talking to your advocates inside the account.

▸ *Key Players.* After the superstar provides an account overview and describes the opportunity and buying process in the strategic plan, she describes the key players. You need to understand all the people involved, their decision-making criteria, and the ranking of those criteria (e.g., is service most important? Or initial purchase price?). An appreciation for the personality types comes in handy when choosing a sales strategy. Who are the key decision makers? Who else will influence the decision? Who are your advocates within the customer organization? What are the specific needs (with prioritization) of each player? If the decision were made today, which way would they go? You need to understand not only the individuals but the complex interactions among them all — the corporate spider web. By the way, who among this stellar cast of characters do you think is the most important person? No, it's not the project leader or even the CEO — it's your key customer contact's executive assistant. The assistant schedules the meetings that you will need to accomplish your objectives. He holds the key to access, so you need to sell him first. Treat him like royalty! I can't emphasize this enough.

▶ ***Solution Differentiation.*** Your strategic plan differentiates your solution from those of your competitors and evaluates it from the customer's perspective. Why are you offering this particular solution? How well does it satisfy the buying criteria of your customer, compared with your competitors' offerings? Finding out the basis upon which the customer will be making her decision is a sales basic. Superstars go farther by asking the customer to rack and stack these purchase criteria — that is, rank them in order of importance.

Secret Weapon 23, the Customer Decision Matrix, is the place to record that information. It is an internal tool (shared only in-house, not with your customer) that allows you to keep tabs on where you stand. Does your solution have a platinum bullet — a unique quality — an unfair advantage (e.g., higher quality, faster speed) that the competing solutions don't have, and that is ranked high in importance by the customer? If you are absolutely sure that this strength matches your customer's criterion, you'd better be highlighting it. In the sample filled-in matrix in Secret Weapon 23, Competitor A's platinum bullet is initial selling price; neither Our Solution nor Competitor B excels in this area, and it is the customer's number one criterion.

Keep in mind that these ratings and criteria rankings are from the initial viewpoint of your customer — not your marketing department. I mention "initial" because one of your strategies may be to dramatically change this matrix (see Change the Game — New Game, later in this chapter).

Eight Major Account Strategies

You have completed most of your strategic plan. Now comes the fun part — choosing a strategy for your account! The strategies are summarized in the table on pages 108–109. Let's discuss each one in detail.

SOLE SOURCE

The Sole Source strategy is appropriate when your company is the only game in town and there are no other contenders in your customer's view. As sales reps we fight for this opportunity but rarely encounter it. It is generally reserved for the true superstar who has achieved the status of trusted advisor, a genuine inside sales consultant. In chapter 1 (see Solver or Avoider, page 15) we described three types of sales reps: the product peddler, the visitor, and the consultative rep, who is

SECRET WEAPON 23

Customer Decision Matrix

This secret weapon is used only in-house. It is not shared with the customer.

Purchase Criterion	Criterion Rank	Our Solution	Competitor A	Competitor B
Initial selling price	1	Poor ★	Excellent ★★★	Poor ★
Service and support	2	Poor ★	Average ★★	Poor ★
Performance	3	Average ★★	Average ★★	Excellent ★★★
Upgradeability	4	Excellent ★★★	Excellent ★★★	Poor ★
Reputation	5	Excellent ★★★	Average ★★	Poor ★

either a problem solver or a problem avoider. The Sole Source strategy is reserved for the rare rep who helps the customer avoid major problems and has therefore earned the right to proceed without competition.

At GE some years ago I identified a potential challenge/opportunity for one of my customers. The State of Illinois Certificate of Need (CON) policy was about to change to make it more difficult for my account to acquire high-tech diagnostic medical equipment. My customer was unaware of this planned course of action. I spoke up, and the customer was most appreciative. By assisting hospital administration very early in the CON process, I helped them avoid what would have been disastrous consequences for the hospital and its bottom line. The customer said, "Thanks for telling me, Dan! Now let's proceed with the purchase. We'll need to contact two of your competitors to get the ball rolling. As you know, we can't make purchases of capital equipment without following our internal policies."

How did I respond? I said, "That's great, Tom. In fact, I would do that, too. I can help you through the process and facilitate matters for you. There are obvious trade-offs, however, to sending the project out for bid. For example, this will push your purchase back by at least six months. After all, you'll have to draft the bid specs, send them out for responses, analyze the bids, and then begin the negotiation process. Based on our previous discussion, that delay may be very costly. We've already agreed that this new purchase will bring in $500,000 per month. If you push the decision out for six months, it will cost you $3 million. Following your

Eight Major Account Strategies

Strategy	Description	When to Deploy
Sole Source	No competition.	▶ When you have earned the right to go it alone as a result of your consultative selling.
Frontal Attack	Blindly facing off against the competition exactly the way the customer tells you to, by agreeing to his or her decision criteria and buying process.	▶ Almost never. In most cases this strategy is a recipe for failure. It should be deployed *only* when your solution, as seen in the eyes of the customer, based on his or her decision criteria, is ten times better than your competitor's.
Change the Game — Expand the Pie	Otherwise known as the Big Bang approach. Make the purchase encompass more than what the customer initially described.	▶ When your competitive position would be improved by expanding the project.
Change the Game — Reduce the Pie	Otherwise known as fractionalizing, or the Trojan horse approach. Make the purchase encompass less than what the customer initially described. Your goal is to first get your foot in the door and then position yourself to win the larger opportunity.	▶ When your competitive position would be improved by pressing ahead with just a piece of the overall project. ▶ When the Big Bang (Expand the Pie) approach carries too much risk.
Change the Game — New Game	Any or all of the following: ▶ Change the relative importance of the current decision criteria. ▶ Add a new criterion to the current criteria and elevate it to top status. ▶ Add or remove steps in the Customer Buying Process. ▶ Add an additional decision maker.	▶ When you are at a competitive disadvantage given the current decision criteria and buying process.

Eight Major Account Strategies (continued)

Strategy	Description	When to Deploy
Accelerate	Speed the buying process.	▶ When you are winning or when something in the future will put you at a competitive disadvantage.
Delay	Delay the buying process.	▶ When you are losing or when something in the future will put you at a competitive advantage. ▶ When you do not have enough information to set a proper strategy.
Disengage	Remove your company and solution from consideration: ▶ Public removal — You phone the customer and send a disengage letter in one last attempt to open communication and properly qualify the opportunity. ▶ Private removal (not recommended) — You do not inform the customer of your disengagement.	▶ When the customer commits an integrity or legal violation such as asking for a kickback. ▶ When you believe that your cost of sale outweighs the benefits of a potential win. ▶ When, despite your repeated attempts to do so, the customer does not permit you to properly qualify the opportunity (BMPCC).

internal policies comes at a price. We are happy to do that, of course, but you should be aware of the opportunity cost of that decision." The customer gave me the order without competition (Sole Source strategy) once I was able to address the issue of competitive pricing by sharing our national account discount structure with him.

Sometimes this strategy works, and sometimes it doesn't. In the worst case, the customer still decides to contact your competitors and you act as his consultant through the entire buying process, resulting in great benefits all the way around. In the best case, you secure a deal with no competitors. For these reasons, the Sole Source strategy is the goal of every superstar.

FRONTAL ATTACK

A Frontal Attack strategy is defined as blindly facing off against your competitors exactly the way the customer tells you to, by agreeing to all of the customer's decision criteria and to her buying process. Most reps use this strategy in error. Remember our discussion earlier, about getting your head beat in by your competitors in the coliseum, while your customer watches? Picture a second warfare scenario: Two rows of armed soldiers lined up on a battlefield across from one another and then marching mindlessly toward each other, with both sides suffering major casualties. Getting on that battlefield makes sense only if your side is armed with machine guns and the other side has squirt guns.

Let's imagine your customer saying, "I want a presentation," or "I need a quote tomorrow," or "I'm going to base my decision on the following criteria: initial cost, image quality, and the number of service engineers within a twenty-mile radius, ranked in that order." What do you do next? Nod and agree? If you agree to the customer's parameters, you are by default agreeing to a Frontal Attack. Perhaps 98% of all sales reps give in to every customer request. After all, traditional sales methods say that customers are always right, and you should give them what they ask for. You'll note that a major piece is missing from this yes-man approach: You did not determine, before you said yes, whether fulfilling the request is in the *best interests of both you and the customer*. If it is not, you work to change the parameters to give you a better chance at winning: You change the buying process, the project time line, the players involved, or the project scope (see Change the Game strategy, below).

If and only if your solution is ten times better than the competition at meeting the customer's buying criteria (to continue the example above, those criteria would be initial cost, image quality, and the number of service engineers within a twenty-mile radius), then knock your socks off and take a Frontal Attack. Accede to every customer request, don't rock the boat, and do whatever the customer asks of you. Remember, though – this is rare.

> ★ SUPERSTAR SECRET ★
>
> **Never fight or argue with a customer. That would be like stepping in front of a speeding train.**

If your solution *doesn't* match those criteria, consider which strategy would be a better fit. You may want to change the buying process, the players involved, or both – perhaps by trying to get someone involved who is currently sitting on the sidelines. Or you may try to change the current buying criteria by changing the customer's rack and stack (that is, the ranking of his purchase criteria) or by adding a brand-new purchase criterion to the mix. You never do this by fighting or arguing with the customer – that would be like standing in front of a speeding train and trying to stop it with your hand. You'll get run over. Instead, you would step off the tracks and say, "Great! I think you are approaching this decision wisely and appropriately. The key criteria you mention are certainly very important to a decision such as the one you are considering. Sometime later I would like to share with you one additional key criterion that Saint Highly Respected Hospital used when they recently made their decision." You are beginning to lay the groundwork to gain trust (climb the left side of the Trust Triangle) and to position a Change the Game – New Game strategy in the future.

Some reps attempt a Frontal Attack based on *misperceptions* about the strength of their product and about the customer's buying criteria. This always leads to a disaster. For instance, GE recently introduced a breakthrough product for cardiovascular imaging. The product offered all the technical bells and whistles you could want. Technically, it was light-years ahead of competitive offerings. GE seemed to be unbeatable. Was it? Of course not. It didn't meet the customer's decision criteria. Many customers wanted to buy from the vendor who was perennially seen as the market share leader. That was Philips, not GE.

Sales reps lose business every day even though their products are superior. This is just another example of the Trust Triangle at work. Decisions are made emotionally, then justified rationally. When GE heralded the new digital mammography system, did GE win every order? Of course not. This was because although GE offered what was arguably the best technology, some customers had different criteria that GE couldn't meet. One customer was constrained by insurmountable budget considerations. GE had the best, but it didn't match his budget. No sale. So it's all about the customer: What is truly important to him?

When I follow this philosophy: My time! My field! My game! And my rules! I am serving the best interests of both my customer and myself. Unless your offering is seen as being ten times better than that of the competition in the eyes of your customer, forget Frontal Attack; choose one of the seven other strategies and play the game *your* way.

The next three strategies are variations on the Change the Game theme. Change the Game comes in three flavors: Expand the Pie, Reduce the Pie, and New Game.

CHANGE THE GAME — EXPAND THE PIE

Expand the Pie, also known as the Big Bang approach, is one of the best strategies you can employ. When your competitive position would be improved by doing so, you expand what the customer is in the market for. You probably have a broad array of products and services available to you. In addition, partnering with other departments in your company allows you to obtain more benefit for your company as well as for the customer. When you expand the pie you simply modify what the customer is buying by adding additional products or services. The customer requests that you provide A; you convince her to consider A, B, C, and D. For example, let's say a customer wants to invest in a new car. The car salesman may have him also consider a special dealer financing opportunity or a unique opportunity to reduce costs by picking up the car in the country in which it is being manufactured: Germany. These additional expand-the-pie offerings are being provided to strengthen the rep's competitive position.

CHANGE THE GAME — REDUCE THE PIE

The next strategy is to reduce, or fractionalize, the pie — otherwise known as the Trojan horse approach. You use Reduce the Pie when your competitive position would be improved by pressing ahead with just a piece of the overall project, or when Expand the Pie carries too much risk. Let's pretend that you're the superstar and I'm your manager. A customer calls you up and says, "We are in the market to buy two CTs, three MRs, two vascular labs, and a catheterization lab for our new center." As your manager, I ask you, "What is your strategy to *win?*" Not just "What is your strategy?" Because we obviously do not want to come in second place on this deal.

In this situation you might consider reducing, or fractionalizing, the pie — pursuing just a piece of the deal first. Let's say your company manufactures the best CT systems around. You have analyzed the customer's product needs and decide to lead with your strength. By focusing on just the CT, you can ride a Trojan horse into the account, demonstrate your product superiority, build trust with the customer, and demonstrate your commitment to serving as her consultant.

You might say to me, "But wait! Didn't I just lose out on the opportunity to sell all that other equipment?" I would argue that you haven't lost anything. You are getting your toe in a door that might have stayed closed to you forever. By deploying a strategy that builds a strong relationship early on, you will be in a better position to win additional business later. You will have a proven success and you will have gained an enormous amount of credibility this way. So which of your products do you lead with? The one that puts you in the best competitive position to beat your competition. Lead with your strongest product.

CHANGE THE GAME — NEW GAME

A great example of Change the Game — New Game can be observed when sports-minded friends argue about which sports figure is better. Someone says, "Who's the best golfer of all time?" And the battle begins. One says "Tiger," one says "Nicklaus." Who is correct? Well, it depends. Just as in a sale, the winner of this argument will be the one who is most adept at persuading the others on what the evaluation criteria should be along with the priority of each criterion. Let's listen in again to this sample argument:

"Nicklaus is obviously the best golfer of all time, because he has won the most victories at the number one tournament in golf, the Masters" (current buying criteria).

"No, Tiger's pace of wins is faster than Nicklaus's and at this rate he will easily surpass Nicklaus. And besides, check out how much money Tiger has made by winning golf tournaments. He's made much, much more than Nicklaus" (Change the Game by adding new criteria).

"No, Nicklaus is best, because when you adjust the winnings for inflation, Nicklaus's winnings far exceed Tiger's" (Change the Game by adding new criteria).

And so the argument (sale) goes on. Only after the two sides agree on the decision criteria and the rack and stack of those criteria will a winner be crowned. Just like selling. The decision criteria can be modified to serve the needs of the sales pro.

You use Change the Game – New Game when you are at a competitive disadvantage given the customer's current decision criteria and buying process. Turn back for a moment to Secret Weapon 23 – Customer Decision Matrix (page 107), which provides a snapshot of the customer's current decision criteria, the rank of those criteria, and each vendor's relative strength – again, in the eyes of the customer. In the example, initial selling price and service/support are ranked first and second in importance by the customer. If you were Competitor B in that matrix, what would be your strategy? Since your solution's performance is considered by the customer to be much better than your competition, your job would be to convince the customer that performance, currently ranked third, deserves a much higher ranking. By changing any or all of the criteria, you've created a New Game.

Another way to start a New Game is by adding a brand-new criterion to the decision and elevating it to high importance in your customer's mind. Let's say that you sell ice machines. You determine through your BMPCC questioning that the customer is ready to invest in a million dollars' worth of ice machines for a major hotel chain. Her purchasing criteria include initial selling price and the volume of ice that can be produced by each machine in one hour. Your company's ice machine has a much higher initial investment and produces ice at only half the speed of your competitor's machine. Based on those buying criteria, you know that if the customer were to make the decision today, you would lose. What is your strategy?

Change the Game to a New Game by convincing the customer that the decibel level of the ice machine and total cost of ownership (TCO) are the two most critical buying criteria. If you have ever spent the night in a hotel room next to an ice machine, you can make an impassioned argument that the volume of ice production pales in importance compared with the machine's decibel level. In fact, the hotel you are working with could actually lose customers if they proceed with the noisy machines, because the rooms next to the ice machines will be undesirable and practically unrentable. Of course you will also educate the customer on the value of considering not just the machines' initial investment but also the total cost of owning them over time. You may highlight your machine's higher trade-in value, your machine's better uptime (reliability), or your lower service costs – or all three.

Let's go back to the example we gave when we were discussing Frontal Attack. Your customer calls and says, "We will buy a CT scanner within a year. I'm going to base my decision on the following criteria: initial cost, image quality, and the number of service engineers within a twenty-mile radius, ranked in that order."

You say, "That sounds great, and it makes sense. Now let's talk about some options you may want to consider." You proceed to Change the Game from checkers to chess by changing the decision criteria. Your company is not going to do well if initial cost is the most important criterion. However, in a TCO analysis, you excel. If you can get the customer to approach the decision from an investment point of view, you can persuade him that the total cost over time is lower after considering the ROI.

With regard to the number of service engineers within twenty miles, let's assume your competitor employs more engineers in the designated area. Do you want to allow this to be a major consideration? No – instead, you want to emphasize the service technology that your company provides to the customer. It's the diagnostic software, after all – not the number of warm bodies – that allows the problem to get fixed. Therefore, it's more important to have the right diagnostic service equipment than to have a technician living nearby.

When you use the Change the Game – New Game strategy you change all, some, or one of the following:

- ▸ Decision makers: Maybe you will expand the decision team to include a strong advocate.

- ▸ Decision criteria: You could change the rack and stack of the current criteria. You could add a new criterion that is not currently being considered and try your best to elevate it to a top criterion.

- ▸ Or you can change the customer's current buying process to one more favorable to your offering.

Which brings us back to the importance of proper account qualification. There is no way for the superstar to select the right strategy unless she knows the customer's decision criteria and how they are ranked, along with the customer's buying process and key decision makers. This is why the BMPCC account qualification best practices we discussed earlier are so important.

ACCELERATE

You employ the Accelerate strategy when you are winning or when something in the future will put you at a competitive disadvantage. If you get a sense that the customer is leaning your way, it's essential that you speed up the decision process to ensure you get the deal. Is there any reason you would want to let the time line stretch out for another six months? No! You need to find a way to abbreviate it. Likewise, if you know that sometime down the line your competitor will be unveiling a snazzy new solution, or your advocate within the customer organization will be retiring, or the price of your product will rise substantially, putting you at a competitive disadvantage, that is also a time to employ the Accelerate strategy.

How does a superstar go about this – in other words, what tactics would she deploy if she chooses the Accelerate strategy? Since you have uncovered the customer's decision process (see D^3, page 45), you already know the time line and you understand which compelling events would justify an acceleration. Once you know the customer's current process, accelerating the process becomes a bit easier: You recommend steps that can be combined or eliminated, thereby shortening the time line. Perhaps getting sign-offs from the IT department and the engineering department could happen simultaneously. Or perhaps the customer can skip the vendor background check if you and the customer have an existing track record.

DELAY

You employ the Delay strategy when you are losing or when something in the future will put you at a competitive advantage. For instance, if your company were about to announce a new product that would be helpful to your customer, you would want to delay the customer's decision until you can provide the product. Or you may also want to temporarily delay the decision so you can gather more information. If you acquire a new account and your manager asks for your strategy, you would have to say, "My strategy is to delay at this point. I need more information. I have to qualify the customer using the BMPCC best practices and learn much more about the key players, decision criteria, and the customer's buying process."

The tactic you would use to deploy this strategy would be to recommend to the customer additional steps that are not currently in the customer's buying process. Perhaps you add an additional customer reference visit, a thorough vendor background check, a solution demonstration, or additional presentations. Once you have gathered the information you need, you choose a different strategy.

DISENGAGE

You will use this last strategy, which is the most controversial, any time you feel it is advisable to pull away from an opportunity. Smaller companies are more aggressive about employing this strategy because they have fewer resources and must guard their expenditures more closely. Larger, more established companies are more likely to go after every opportunity because they have larger budgets. No matter what the size of your company, you can save your company money and save yourself time by learning when to disengage.

You don't disengage because the customer won't return your calls, or because he cancels two site visits, or because he's occasionally annoying. Disengagement requires a more powerful reason. If he continually refuses to share essential information that would allow you to qualify him, you would be well advised to bow out. Perhaps he has discussed the fact that the project is budgeted, but won't tell you anything else. This leaves you unable to determine the viability of the sale.

You owe it to your company to minimize its cost of sales, and if you are unable to do so, your company can't be expected to speculate further. If you truly feel that the customer cannot provide a return on your cost of sales, you would be wise to withdraw from the opportunity. If a customer commits an integrity violation, such as asking for a kickback on the deal, this also brings about a quick disengagement.

There are two ways to employ the Disengage strategy. You can disengage privately — that is, not inform the customer that you are withdrawing — perhaps in the hope that by staying in the game, however loosely, you may still win the deal. A private disengagement is not recommended. Stay in or get out — but be clear with the customer where you stand.

When you disengage publicly you phone the customer and send a disengage letter (**Secret Weapon 24**) in one last attempt to open communication and properly qualify the account. A word to the wise: Deciding to disengage is a major decision. It could be career threatening to make this move alone! Include your manager and avoid "special assignment" in this very important decision (see The Lone Ranger Is Dead, page 137).

Your disengage letter should explain your decision to the customer in polite, direct, unapologetic terms: "It appears that our company has not earned the right to work as your vendor at this time, but we are hopeful there may be an opportunity to work together in the future." When used correctly, a disengage letter can help you gain tremendous credibility. In a large percentage of cases, the customer will

SECRET WEAPON 24

Disengage Letter

Lindsay Johnson
Senior Vice President
Baker Corporation
32434 State Street
Montpelier, VT 05602

Dear Lindsay:

Thank you for requesting that we provide a proposal on your new system.

Based upon our perception of Baker Corporation's level of interest in a thorough evaluation of Adams & Associates' solutions, it is apparent that we have not earned the right to work with you on this project. Out of respect for your time, we are withdrawing from consideration.

Though naturally disappointed that we will be removed from your consideration, we look forward to earning the right to work with you on your next project.

Please contact me if my team can be of any assistance to you during the design, installation, and training stages of your project.

I wish you the best of luck as Baker Corporation begins the challenging and rewarding process of expanding its services.

Sincerely,

Ben

Benjamin Edwards
cell 630-555-1212

call and ask you not to withdraw. The superstar knows that this is a time for quid pro quo. Yes, you say, we would be delighted to reengage in the opportunity if the customer agrees to certain conditions, such as making available to you the key decision makers, answering the BMPCC questions, and perhaps delaying the decision until you can gather the information you need.

Turn back one last time to Secret Weapon 23 – Customer Decision Matrix on page 107. Now that you know all eight strategies, which one would you recommend for the company in the Our Solution column? If you represent Our Solution, what is your strategy to win, and why did you select that specific strategy? The customer gives your upgradeability and reputation excellent grades, but those criteria are ranked fourth and fifth – not first or second. So it would be your job to Change the Game to a New Game, one in which the criteria at which you excel – upgradeability and reputation – are moved from a lower rank to a higher rank. Why? As always, the answer is that it puts you in a better competitive position to win.

What if you are the sales rep for Competitor A? What is your strategy to win? It appears that Competitor A is leading in the criterion that the customer *currently* ranks first (initial selling price). Would you choose a Frontal Attack? We said earlier that the Frontal Attack should be used *only* when, in the eyes of the customer, you have a solution ten times better than the competition. From the limited information given so far, it's impossible to determine if a Frontal Attack is the best strategy. If I were a rep for Competitor A, I would employ an Accelerate strategy and get the deal while the getting's good.

What if you are Competitor B, most of whose criteria are considered by the customer to be downright poor? As Competitor B, you are in trouble: You get low marks in all the customer's decision criteria except performance. What is your strategy to win? Competitor B must not fall into the trap of deploying a Frontal Attack, no matter what. In addition to changing the customer's rack and stack, mentioned earlier, Competitor B could try a Delay strategy to bring in additional decision criteria that would create a distinct competitive advantage over the other two vendors. Competitor B must then convince the customer that these new purchase criteria should be pushed to the very top ranking. In addition, Competitor B could consider changing or adding a key decision maker, or changing the customer's buying process.

Choosing Your Tactics

Once a strategy is selected, you detail the tactics necessary to deploy the strategy. The action items should include the person responsible and the date by which the item will be completed. Your tactic document might read something like this:

Tactics

Action	Owner	Date	Complete
Set up meeting with Jill Smith to review service history	Adams	July 1	No
Schedule meeting with my boss and CFO to discuss financial options	Adams	August 8	No

Keep in mind, though, that 90% of the game is execution! Great execution will overcome bad strategy every day of the week. And great relationships trump poor tactics and poor strategy. If you can't identify the key players in the account, or understand the relationships at the top level of the company, you will probably lose the deal, even if you select the perfect strategy.

Superstar selling is based on a foundation of credibility and concern for the customer. Its proper execution mandates the development of relationships at the highest levels of the customer organization. Therefore, one of your tactics should be an executive relationship plan for your accounts. You need to have some way for you and your managers to interface with your customer's key executives, and that is hard to do without key business relationships. Put a plan together to allow for this networking; you will be rewarded in the long term.

▶ Step 4 — Providing Proof and Justification ◀

You've chosen your strategy and outlined your tactics. What now? At this stage in the customer's buying process the customer is evaluating vendors, which is your opportunity to prove the superiority of your offering and justify the customer's decision to go with your solution.

Providing Proof from the Inside

At every step in the customer's buying process you look for opportunities to help the customer by acting as her consultant. You scout for potential headaches in an effort to avoid them. Vendor presentations can be headache-makers for customers: The vendors don't stick to the time allotted for the presentation, they stray from desired topics, and the presentations themselves do not occur in a short time window. Consequently, after the demonstration the customer cannot even remember the differences between vendors A, B, and C.

If the customer needs it, the superstar steps in and volunteers templates for communicating to vendors the protocol and suggested content for the event. Turn back for a moment to Secret Weapon 10 – Presentation Protocol Letter on page 63. Draft a similar letter and offer it to your customer as a possible tool for her use.

Likewise, a customer new to making such a large purchase might not know how to evaluate the presentations when they occur. You, as the superstar, have been there, done that hundreds of times, and can assist the customer. See Secret Weapon 11 – Presentation Report Card on page 64. Create a similar card for your customer's use, with the Grade and Comments columns left blank.

So here we have the irony of being a superstar consultative rep working closely with the customer to meet the customer's needs: By helping the customer document his buying process (also see Secret Weapons 12 and 13, the Request for Proposal Cover Letter and Request for Proposal Excerpt) you are simultaneously helping to fulfill the proof and justification step of your sales process. A further irony is that you will be teaching the customer how to set up not only your own sales presentations but those of your competitors, and helping the customer decide how to evaluate these presentations. I believe this is called sitting in the catbird seat.

At all times, however, be mindful about *never* destroying the trust that your customer has placed in you by slanting in your favor the documents you are providing. To maintain trust, all these tools should be generic.

Presentation Skills

You've helped the customer set the stage for the presentations by you and your competitors. What happens now? Let's cover some superstar basics. Your overall goal is to differentiate yourself in a positive way in the eyes of the customer, especially as compared with your competition. Prior to the meeting, call or visit each key attendee in the customer organization and say something like this: "Hi, this is Dan with Adams & Associates. Thank you very much for agreeing to attend my presentation next week. Your time is extremely valuable and I want to make sure I use it as efficiently as possible. Could we please review the top three points that you would like me to cover during my presentation?" After the customer tells you the three points, you ask, "Could you please prioritize those three objectives?" Now that you know these three points, you have an opportunity to Change the Game in your favor by suggesting additional topics that the customer has not volunteered.

> **★ SUPERSTAR SECRET ★**
>
> Use customer quotes in your slide presentations. People love seeing their ideas broadcast in bright lights.

What are the obvious topics that you will cue up with your customer? Your unfair advantages. This is called prepositioning your unfair advantages. You are simply getting confirmation from the customer that he has a need for your unfair advantage while getting permission to review it during your formal presentation.

During this conversation you take detailed notes on your customer comments so that you can customize your presentation outline to your customer and even use some of his comments to hammer home your key unfair advantages. This customized outline, summarized on one of the first slides in your presentation, should help you gain enormous credibility.

Before you get to your unfair advantages, though, use a credibility preface in the form of a slide that contains a customer quote. For example, let's imagine that in the pre-presentation customer conference the customer said, "The reliability of the equipment is my most important purchasing consideration." You would use this quote immediately before discussing your powerful servicing capabilities. This works every time! People love seeing their ideas broadcast in bright lights. The quote will also highlight the customer's need for your unfair advantage.

> ### ★ SUPERSTAR SECRET ★
> **When making a presentation, you always, always, *always* want to go last.**

If you are competing against two other vendors, and you have the opportunity to choose the timing of your presentation, which do you choose: first, second, or third? For a superstar the answer is all three. How is this possible? You go first and second informally by meeting with your customer and presenting one-on-one prior to your competitor's first-slot presentation. As we discussed earlier, the superstar never directly criticizes the competition; instead, you discuss the trade-offs of the various options. So in this informal meeting you would focus on trade-offs in order to contain the effect of your competitors' unfair advantages.

You always, always, *always* want to go last — whether it's a site visit, product evaluation, presentation, demonstration, or negotiation. Being last provides several advantages: (1) You get a sense of what the competitors are saying about you and their solutions prior to your presentation. (2) You can diffuse any perceived limitations of your solution during your presentation, and close the customer. (3) There is strong research to suggest that customers remember the last word.

Try to control the presentation logistics. Customers frequently dictate where the presentation will be held. The superstar knows that when this happens the customer is asking you to jump into the Roman coliseum and play the game his way. This is a recipe for disaster. Remember: My time! My field! My game! My rules! The location may not be conducive to your cause. It may be too small, stuffy, noisy, poorly lit, or simply unsuitable from an audiovisual standpoint. Thoroughly investigate the location in advance to ensure your satisfaction with the room itself. If the facilities are not satisfactory, you must Change the Game to a New Game and find a better location.

The executive assistant responsible for setting up the presentations may balk at helping you find an alternative: "The other vendors found nothing wrong with the basement conference room." My response would be, "Great. I'm glad that worked out for them. Given all we plan to review with your team, however, it would not be in their best interests to use the current location." A colleague used this technique to his advantage when negotiating a huge software deal for his company. "I knew my two major competitors had both presented in the designated room," he said, "which was small and a bit stuffy. It would have actually been OK. Instead, I asked for a different room, one that was larger and more airy – just to stand out. The selection of this forum alone raised the bar and succeeded in differentiating me and my company."

This sort of account guidance allows you to modify and control the customer's buying process to not only serve the customer but also meet your needs.

Pricing

The phone rings. It's your customer calling to say, "I need a quote tomorrow morning on your highest-quality product. Can you get that to me?" How do you respond? This situation is another superstar turning point – an STP. A typical rep would rush back to his office, yell for his specialist, and burn the midnight oil churning out a fifty-five-page response. He would toss in a brochure and probably a national discount, throw it at the customer, and cross his fingers.

> ### ★ SUPERSTAR SECRET ★
> **The goal in pricing is to position yourself as a consultant in the quote process and delay providing formal pricing as long as possible.**

A superstar knows it is never in his best interest to provide formal pricing early in the game. Our goal in pricing is to delay providing a formal final price as long as possible. Providing a formal final price one week into a seven-month buying process is *very* bad. You don't even know exactly what the customer needs, and whether, in fact, your solution is the right one for the customer. Earlier I invited you to empathize with the customer by imagining the customer as your mother. Would you just dump equipment on your Mom? Even assuming that your solution is right for your customer, if you provide detailed pricing now, that means that in months 5, 6, and 7 you will have to provide pricing again in response to additional customer requests. At that point you will be competing against yourself – your prior pricing bids. So the goal is to give the customer just enough to satisfy his budget process – a letter quote at list price (**Secret Weapon 25** – Budgetary Pricing Letter and **Secret Weapon 26** – Budgetary Pricing Proposal).

I was beaten up badly several times over the years. Early on I was a quote machine. Average reps adhere to this motto: "When in doubt, quote!" Most companies do a great job of teaching their reps their administrative duties. They don't do a very good job of teaching high-quality consultative and strategic selling skills. After my initial sales training, I could churn out bids better than anybody. The quotes were usually numbered, with a letter suffix. I would start out with "A"; the quote would get altered so many times that if I was lucky enough to get the sale, the final quote would end in "Z". It was of no value to me to quote this way.

Ultimately you will probably have to generate quotes, but it should be at the end of your sales process. In fact, you should adopt the mindset that you will *never* quote. Instead, as a courtesy to the customer who is trying to put together a budget, you can provide budgetary quotes and use the opportunity to act as a consultant to your customer. Of course, you will have to provide a detailed quote eventually – so the "never" isn't accurate. But you want to put it off as long as possible.

> ★ **SUPERSTAR SECRET** ★
>
> **Adopt the mindset that you will *never* quote.**

The customer pushes back and says, "Your competitor is doing it – why won't you?" You can respond a number of ways. First, you could say, "Well, are you ready to invest right now? If not, then why do you need a formal contract? It really wouldn't be in your best interest to generate contracts at this point." Second, there are legal repercussions. "A quote is a formal legal document, and our respective lawyers would have to review it. Are you at that stage?" Third, you insert a time limit. "Our bids are valid for only thirty days, after which they expire." Fourth, as circumstances change, discounts change. "You are not at that point yet, as I understand it." Finally, you remind the customer that it is rare to receive every dollar requested in a budget. You say, "Mr. Customer, you have not fully developed your budget needs, because you haven't decided on your product options. If you take your bid to your CFO now, you'll be stuck with that number and you may be unable to obtain the options you want."

Most important, use this customer request as an STP – a chance to distinguish yourself as a true consultant to the customer. This way you begin to establish credibility and position yourself as a consultant drafting the proposal specifications, which will allow you to guide the buying process.

"Mr. Customer, let me say, respectfully, that I think you will bring on a major headache if you request quotes from vendors without a fair bidding process. I

SECRET WEAPON 25

Budgetary Pricing Letter

Lee Gannon
Senior Vice President
ABC Corporation
18 Thorndike Road
Wakefield, MA 01880

Dear Lee:

> When a qualified customer requests formal pricing too early in the buying process, you would be wise to not drop everything and crank out a 55-page response. Instead, provide a quick quote highlighting your unfair advantages. Then assist the customer in putting together bid specifications (Secret Weapons 12 and 13) that will actually provide the information he needs.

Thank you for considering our equipment for your new Imaging System project.

Attached is the formal pricing you requested for our full-featured MedCT 1400. You will see that most of the options for this system have been included in the price.

Designed for speed and cost savings, the system offers:

► [Unfair Advantage 1]
► [Unfair Advantage 2]
► [Unfair Advantage 3]

I look forward to assisting you with this exciting new Imaging System project.

Sincerely,

Ben

Benjamin Edwards
cell 630-555-1212

SECRET WEAPON 26

Budgetary Pricing Proposal

Pricing Proposal

Prepared for:
Lee Gannon
Senior Vice President
ABC Corporation
18 Thorndike Road
Wakefield, MA 01880

This budgetary pricing proposal, provided early in the buying process only at the customer's request, gives basic information and quotes your solution's full price. Do not waste time on detailed pricing proposals until late in the sales process.

System:
Single-plane MedCT 1400

Includes:
▶ Omega V Table
▶ User-configurable tableside controls
▶ Dual monitor support
▶ 3-axis MedCT C-arm
▶ Digital system
▶ Digital flat panel detector

Benefits:
▶ 3-axis Gantry flexibility
▶ Unsurpassed image quality
▶ Ultra low-dose
▶ High-speed spin technology
▶ Ergonomic controls provide ease of use

Total investment: $1,500,000

can help you avoid that headache." Offer to provide a template for a request for proposal cover letter (Secret Weapon 12) and a detailed request for proposal (excerpted in Secret Weapon 13) so the customer will have an apples-to-apples comparison of the various options. If he balks, give him references where other customers tried to simply ask for bids and were burned by the chaos: The vendors played games, the customers did not get what they wanted, and so on. "You know, the CEO down the street just did what you are planning to do. After he received the three quotes, he spent hours on the weekend trying to compare the bids. It was a huge headache for him." Then share with the customer a chaos-free example or two of how things worked out beautifully using your RFP and cover letter templates.

True or false: Given the opportunity to help the customer with bid specs, you should fill the document with specifications that lock out your competition. Let's assume you've been granted the opportunity to help draft the specs. Would a superstar slant all the specs in favor of his company? An average rep – yes. A superstar – never! It goes to credibility. Your customer has just placed great trust in you by allowing you this kind of participation. If slanted bid specs are sent out, what do you think the competitors will do when they receive them? They will call senior executives in the customer organization to complain. Your customer could lose his job.

A superstar knows it is crucial that the specs always stay generic (unless the customer specifically requests lockout specs, as in the case of government accounts that are required to buy from the lowest bidder). Having said that, I will now share with you that in almost all circumstances when I assisted customers with their specs, they were in fact slanted toward my company. How is this possible? Think about the process of working together to draft specs. Step by step you walk the customer through the template to customize it. This provides the opportunity to ask the customer about his needs every step of the way. You can talk with your customer about features and benefits he eventually decides to include in the bid. You can explore why that feature is important to him. Typically, you reach a point where you say, "Mr. Customer, I agree with your selection of that option, but I want to advise you that while we offer that option, Vendor B does not. If that's your choice, this part of the bid will lock her out."

You can't lose by saying this. In many cases the customer responds by saying, "I realize that, but that feature is so important that I want to include it in the bid specifications." You have gained credibility by mentioning the possible bias. In addition, you may have affirmed the customer's desire to select your product, which happens to include the feature mentioned.

Selling Value

True or false: A superstar sells value by highlighting the financial impact of her solution's unique unfair advantages. What is value? Simply, it is what is left after you subtract all the costs from all the benefits. In determining value I picture an iceberg. When customers evaluate the various solutions to their business challenges, they often consider only the costs and revenue streams that are apparent at the time of purchase. They typically consider total selling price, which says nothing about the costs that lie ahead. The initial cost is the part of the iceberg visible above water; quite frequently, the costs below water – the TCO – are substantially larger.

A superstar does indeed sell value by highlighting the hard-dollar impact of her unique unfair advantages. You must be able to quantify, in hard dollars, why your customer should invest more for your solution than that of your competitors based on either a lower TCO or a higher ROI. When the customer says, "Hey! Your competitor's price is much lower than yours," your job is to point out the portion of the iceberg that's below the surface.

To prove a lower TCO or higher ROI, highlight how your unfair advantages result in reduced costs, increased revenue, improved quality, improved productivity, increased efficiency, or some combination there-of. Each of these drivers affects net income and earnings per share by increasing total revenues, decreasing total costs, or both.

> ★ **SUPERSTAR SECRET** ★
>
> **Sell value by highlighting the hard-dollar impact of your solution's unique unfair advantages.**

Let's use an example. Vendor A's solution has a selling price of $4.6 million and Vendor B's is $5.0 million. Which is the better investment? If the sales reps for Vendor A and Vendor B are average reps and not superstars, the decision is simple: Vendor A is cheaper, so it wins. But if Vendor B is represented by a superstar who clearly shows that her solution has a track record of achieving a $600,000 advantage over Vendor A when the trade-in value is taken into consideration, then Vendor B wins.

Here's another example: Why do I spend $100 per year for my American Express Gold Card when I can get a MasterCard for free? I remember the call I received from the American Express sales rep. Within sixty seconds she had convinced me that the card was worth much more than my $100 investment. She did this by documenting the savings and services I would receive as a result of using the card. Likewise, you may be able to say to your customer, "Yes, we're going to be 10% higher. But I'm going to justify why we are worth 50% more at the end of the day."

SECRET WEAPON 27

Selling Value Matrix

Unfair Advantage	Function	Benefit	Proof	Show Me the Money! (Specifically, why should a customer pay more because of this unfair advantage?)
Ultra-fast reconstruction time	Allows for faster processing	Permits higher throughput	ROI analysis, reference quotes	One additional procedure per day equates to $378,900/year in additional revenue

Think about your solution's unfair advantages and how they translate into hard-dollar impacts on your customer's bottom line. Fill out **Secret Weapon 27,** the Selling Value Matrix, for your solution.

Value-Added Matrix

When concentrating on selling value, beware of becoming column fodder. Late in the customer's buying process the customer usually finds value in analyzing the difference between your product and the competitors'. This makes sense – the customer needs details, facts, and sound reasoning – not just for himself but to provide justification, if needed, to any decision makers higher up in the organization. To ply your customer with generalities such as "Our product is way better" won't cut it.

If your customer begins to prepare a comparison matrix, he is creating a way to compare you against your competitors. It indicates he is making a price-sensitive decision and is about to commoditize his choice. The only time you want to see column fodder is when *you* prepare it. A superstar sales rep anticipates this customer need and creates a value-added matrix, which provides that justification while helping the rep sell value. **Secret Weapon 28** is one such value-added matrix, put together during the sale of a CT system to a hospital. It helped the CFO analyze the difference between our product and the competitor's.

When you create your Value-Added Matrix to quantify the hard-dollar value of your unfair advantages, be careful to give credit to your competitors' value in addition to your own. A key point: It is rare that a benefit lasts only one year. Be sure to project your solution's added value for each year into the future. For example, if your solution provides an annual dollar value of $100,000 over your competition, and your customer will use your solution for five years, be sure to quantify the total value ($500,000) of this benefit.

> ★ **SUPERSTAR SECRET** ★
>
> **A customer objection is a gift handed to you on a silver platter — the chance to differentiate yourself as a superstar.**

The value-added matrix that you might create for a customer will look different, depending on your industry and your customer's needs. You will still, however, need to be totally on top of the details of your competitors' offerings. Preparing a Value-Added Matrix will help you to consistently sell value and earn a higher selling price for your solution.

Vaporizing Objections

To an average sales rep, handling objections effectively is the hardest thing to do. To a superstar rep, the opportunity couldn't be sweeter! First of all, the superstar knows that an objecting customer is a good thing — it means the customer is interested enough in the superstar's solution to talk about it. Second, an objecting customer is handing something to you on a silver platter: another STP — a chance to differentiate yourself as a sales superstar. You can use my Objection Vaporizer to gain the customer's trust and proceed hand-in-hand toward a win-win solution. Here are the seven simple steps:

1. Anticipate the objections
2. Confirm the issue
3. Use a credibility preface
4. Confirm the underlying need
5. Apply the Objection Vaporizer
6. Confirm that the customer is comfortable with your response
7. Segue to the sale

SECRET WEAPON 28

Value-Added Matrix

	Our System	Competitor's System	Our Financial Advantage
Trade-in credit	Allows for future upgrade to current, which includes deinstallation of existing system at no cost. Higher future resale value.	Not included.	The value of the product 10 years later = $75,000.
Value	$75,000	$0	$75,000
Installation	Average, 2–4 days; 2-day weekend installation can be negotiated (~3 days faster than competitor).	Average, 5–7 days; self-leveling epoxy floor takes 2 days to dry.	57% faster installation gets you operational faster = $28,800 in 1st year additional potential revenue.
Value	$28,800	$0	$28,800
Tube life and tube replacement time	Average tube life, 21 months; 3 hours to replace.	Average tube life, 9–12 months; 15 hours to replace (assume 9 during business hours).	Our tubes last almost twice as long = $14,400 additional potential revenue in 1st year.
Value	$0	−$14,400	$14,400
Scheduled preventive maintenance downtime	4 hours per quarter (assume 4 business hours) = 16 hours/year.	8 hours per month (assume 8 business hours) = 96 hours/year.	83% less scheduled downtime = $128,000 additional potential revenue in 1st year.
Value	$25,600	−$153,600	$128,000
Productivity consulting	6-week consulting engagement included in service contract.	Not available.	Written guarantee to reduce variability in health care = $50,000 additional guaranteed revenue in 1st year.
Value	$50,000	$0	$50,000

SECRET WEAPON 28 (continued)

Value-Added Matrix

	Our System	Competitor's System	Our Financial Advantage
Remote monitoring, analysis, reporting, and servicing	Broadband monitoring included in service contract; more than 70% of issues closed or partially resolved remotely.	Not available.	Increased and more efficient equipment utilization = $38,000 additional potential revenue in 1st year.
Value	$38,000	$0	$38,000
CT productivity features	Exclusive productivity features.	Not available.	Saving just 30 seconds per exam can allow 1 or more additional patient scans/day = $100,000 additional potential revenue in 1st year.
Value	$100,000	$0	$100,000
Marketing & press kit	Designed to target referring physicians and patients with customizable media-ready materials.	Unknown.	Advertising value of marketing & press kits.
Value	$85,000	$0	$85,000
Trade-in value at 48 months	~32% of original market value in 4 years.	~20% of original market value in 4 years.	62% higher resale value in 4 years.
Value	$320,000	$200,000	$120,000
Total additional added financial value provided by our system			$639,200

ANTICIPATE OBJECTIONS

Step 1 in handling any objection is to ensure that you are never surprised and therefore never defensive. Work with your marketing department or find a veteran rep who can help determine the top five objections you may be facing. Research! Put yourself in your customer's shoes and ask what might be undesirable about the proposed solution. Role-play until you are very comfortable addressing each objection. Even the most complex and technical products and solutions end up having only a handful of key objections. Don't worry about objections – look forward to them! I was always surprised how even the most technical of products brought up only a handful of customer objections, which I could anticipate and learn to address.

CONFIRM THE ISSUE (QUESTIONS ARE THE ANSWERS)

Step 2 in addressing objections is to thoroughly understand your customer's articulated issue. Let's say your customer gives you the standard "your price is too high" objection. If you are an average rep, you sprint back to your manager and request an additional ten points of discount. Your manager is already at her discount limit, so she must call corporate headquarters to obtain permission for the deep discount. After receiving a yes from the CEO, your manager calls you at home with the great news. The next morning, you dart into your customer's office to excitedly announce, "I got the additional discount you requested on the equipment. When can we get the purchase order?" The customer smiles and says, "Thank you very much for that, but I was referring to your maintenance and support costs being out of line. While I appreciate your help on the equipment side, what can you do for me on the maintenance and support?"

Ouch! Let this happen to you more than once and you will be put on "special assignment." Why did this scenario occur? It is simply because you failed to ask questions that would clarify the customer's objection.

Question your customer fully. Ask for his help in understanding every aspect of his objection. Your job might be to redefine price in the customer's mind (Change the Game strategy). Price is not the initial cost of a product or solution but rather the *total cost of ownership* of that solution over time. Price may also be redefined as *return on investment*. What will be the returns to the customer's organization from this product or solution?

USE A CREDIBILITY PREFACE

When a customer presents an objection, you have two options. Fight him and tell him he is wrong, or use the circumstance to gain credibility. Remember the train track? A train is roaring straight at you. Your customer is riding the train with his objection in tow. You try to stop the oncoming objection by standing on the tracks with your hand up, demanding that the train screech to a halt. Given the train's weight and rate of speed, we all know this is impossible. The result would not be pretty. I can still hear my mentor, Sam, telling me during my training program at GE, "Dan, get off the tracks!"

Your other option is to simply step out of the way – allow the train to whiz by. But by all means, jump on the caboose. Work your way through the cars and up to the conductor, where you can eventually convince him to change tracks in your favor. A credibility preface (step 3) allows you to step off the tracks and prevent a confrontation with the train/customer. The simplest credibility preface to use with most objections is to say, "I can understand why you'd feel that way. I would also feel that way, if I were you." Simply agreeing that a customer has a right to make an objection helps to diffuse the customer's discomfort and creates a feeling of trust between you and the customer.

After acknowledging your customer's position, ask yourself whether the customer is misinformed or correct. If he is indeed misinformed, you can gently correct him with unbiased proof of your position. Be delicate – correcting a customer is risky business, and you should do so only if you believe he can see the error. If the customer's objection is sound and well based in fact, you move to step 4.

CONFIRM THE UNDERLYING NEED

Step 4 is your most important step in handling objections. You must uncover the underlying need that is causing the customer's objection. Let's say you are selling cars. Your potential buyer walks in and says, "I don't like that car. It doesn't have enough horsepower." You provide a credibility preface, by responding, "It's true that there are cars out there with more horsepower than this one." Then you ask, "Can you tell me why horsepower is so important to you?" (You are seeking the underlying need.) She says, "I need to accelerate quickly for passing on the highway." Now you can respond: "So what you are really looking for is speed and responsiveness." In other words, you have identified her real need as performance.

In my experience, there are typically six high-level needs for most business-to-business purchases:

- ► Performance/quality
- ► Ease of use
- ► Reliability/service
- ► Upgradeability
- ► ROI/TCO
- ► Risk reduction

As each of the first five needs gets met, the perceived risk of the purchase *decreases* for the customer.

APPLY THE OBJECTION VAPORIZER™

Now that you have uncovered your customer's underlying needs, you are in a position to use step 5, the Objection Vaporizer — a matrix that integrates your customer's high-level needs with your company's unfair advantages, allowing you to immediately address your customer's stated needs. **Secret Weapon 29** shows an Objection Vaporizer for a car sale. Can you guess what you should say to the car-shopping customer?

Find the column that is important to your customer and share your unfair advantages that are related to her key need. Since her need is performance, for instance, you would focus on superior handling, dynamic stability control, acceleration, Turbo-boost, and braking distance. "Ms. Customer, since performance is a priority for you, let me highlight just a few of this car's advantages — which are exclusive to our line. We provide something called Turbo-boost. Even though this car doesn't have as much horsepower as some others, its Turbo-boost allows you to accelerate from 0 to 60 in four seconds! This car's responsiveness is unparalleled, thanks to its aerodynamics and design."

SECRET WEAPON 29

Objection Vaporizer

	Performance/ Quality	Ease of Use	Reliability/ Service	Upgrade-ability	ROI/TCO	Risk Reduction
Unfair Advantages	Superior handling	Auto door lock	10-year warranty	Great trade-in value	Excellent trade-in value	Largest market share
	Dynamic stability control	Dashboard controls	Free car washes	No-cost software upgrades	No-cost software upgrades	Local dealership supported by community
	Acceleration: 0 to 60 in 4 seconds	Hands-free motorized rear door	Home pick-up and drop-off		10-year warranty	
	Turbo-boost	Smart key recognition system	Computer-controlled maintenance indicator			
	Braking distance					

If you fail to meet all the customer's needs with the performance-related unfair advantages, you turn to the unfair advantages in the other columns. For example, you stress the car's high trade-in value and the model's large market share, in addition to mentioning the car's performance.

CONFIRM CUSTOMER COMFORT

Step 6 in handling objections is to make sure you have addressed her concerns. Simply ask, "Have I been able to address your needs to your satisfaction?" If the answer is no, then you will discover another aspect of the objection that you can discuss. If you have satisfied the objection, you have achieved a significant accomplishment. You have made the customer feel that you care about and are able to thoroughly respond to her worries. In other words, you have earned her trust.

SEGUE TO THE SALE ("BY THE WAY...")

Now that you have succeeded in meeting your customer's objections, you can segue into other matters, bringing you closer to your sale. An effective way to move on to the issue at hand is to simply use the transition statement: "By the way, have we discussed your delivery requirements for this car?" That's the seventh and final handling-objections step.

Negotiation Best Practices

Imagine for a moment that you are preparing for a heated final negotiation to secure a very important deal for your company. Your customer asks you to lower your price by X dollars in return for the deal. What do you do? Should you bring in your manager to assist? What will prevent your customer from taking your negotiated offer and sitting on it forever? Or worse, what if your customer allows the expiration date of the offer to come and go but still requires the negotiated deal? In twenty years of selling I've honed my theories of successful negotiations into fifteen commandments. The commandments are easy to comprehend, but following them requires sales discipline.

MAKE SURE THEY ARE READY

Do not negotiate if the customer is not ready to buy. You will end up negotiating two, three, four, or more times. If you drop the price any time before the final negotiation, you will end up competing against yourself – a major mistake.

A rep who does not have a good command of D^3 will sometimes offer to drop the price of his offering in return for a quick order. Most of the time, though, the customer is not ready to move mountains to give the rep the order, so the answer is no sale. The only thing the rep has accomplished by offering to drop the price is a severe negative impact on the final sell price, because now all future price negotiations will begin at the low *quick deal price*. This disaster can be prevented if the rep has a good handle on exactly what steps lie ahead for the customer and if he can rationally assess with his manager this specific customer's amenability to a *quick deal*. Never offer a quick deal price unless you're 99.99% sure it will be immediately accepted.

NEGOTIATE ONLY WITH DECISION MAKERS

Refuse to negotiate with people who do not have the ultimate decision-making authority. I have lost deals – and wasted a lot of time – from making this mistake. Make sure the person you're talking to has the power to say yes.

KNOW YOUR CUSTOMER

Do your homework. Make sure you know the personalities of all the players, both your customer's and your competitor's.

ANALYZE THE COMPETITION

Know as much as possible about your top competitors. What has been their sales strategy? What solutions have they offered? At what price? And with what terms?

REVIEW ALL POSSIBLE SCENARIOS

Know all possible moves that the customer may make. Plan your move in each instance. This will allow you to anticipate the possible scenarios.

KNOW YOUR WALK-AWAY POSITION

Be prepared to eliminate yourself from the negotiation, if necessary. Review the circumstances under which it would be necessary to walk away.

PREPARE A TRADE MATRIX

A trade matrix (**Secret Weapon 30**) ensures that you have planned ahead for a successful negotiation. In private – the customer never sees this matrix – you anticipate what might happen during the negotiations and what your responses will be. In column 1, Give, you list all the items on which you could give a little, such as price, warranty terms, delivery timing, training, education, options, software, upgrades, and so on.

In column 2, Value, you assign a dollar value to each of the Give items. Remember, nothing is free. If you decide to give something to your customer, you must first make sure that he is well aware of its value. What if something – a quick delivery, for instance – has no price? The superstar finds a way to calculate the cost (to the superstar) and the value (to the customer) of providing quick delivery.

SECRET WEAPON 30

Trade Matrix

Give	Value	Get	Can't Touch This!
Extended Warranty	$30,000	▸ THE ORDER!	▸ Access to software code
Fast Delivery	$50,000	▸ Extended warranty	▸ License agreements
Extended Payment Terms	$20,000	▸ Multiple orders rather than a single order	▸ Deep price discount
Fast Installation	$10,000		
Training	$12,000	▸ Sole Source agreement on next purchase	**This internal tool is never shared with the customer — just with your manager.**
Accessories	TBD		
Options	TBD	▸ Positive reference	
Consumables	TBD	▸ Improved payment terms	

In column 3, Get, you list the items you would like the customer to give to you. At the top would be a formal, contingency-free purchase order accompanied by a down payment. Other items in the Get column could include a long-term support agreement, accelerated payment terms, executive access, reference site status (many customers want to be a positive reference for other potential customers), and financing.

In the last column you list the items that the customer might request of you but that are strictly nonnegotiable, such as software license agreements, the software code, and any request that could be deemed an integrity violation (for example, kickbacks, illegal requests, lying, and side letters).

THE LONE RANGER IS DEAD

After you compile the trade matrix, review it in detail with your manager long before the negotiations begin. A superstar never conducts a major final negotiation alone. There are many reasons for this:

▸ Customers do not believe that a sales rep has the authority to produce a great deal. Whatever the actual truth might be, they think that unless a manager is involved, they will not get a bottom-line deal.

▸ Two sets of eyes and ears can better pick up the all-important nonverbal cues coming from the customer.

▶ The negotiations can get heated. By allowing the manager, at times, to take on the bad-guy role, the superstar can keep his relationship with the customer untarnished ("I wish I could give that to you, but my management won't allow it").

▶ Throughout the buying process the superstar has told the customer that the pricing provided is the very best she can do. If the superstar, in response to the "your price is too high" objection, suddenly indicates that she now has the flexibility to lower the price, this calls into question her integrity. The manager is there to quietly make any necessary concessions and close the deal.

▶ Should a superstar negotiate the big deal? In my opinion, no — for the reason mentioned above. In addition, many customers want to discuss price much too early. The superstar can tell the customer that he does not control price, and add, "At the appropriate time, my manager will assist us in reaching a mutually agreeable total investment that is tailored to your needs."

HANDLE THE PRICE OBJECTION

When the price objection is raised, you have to find out whether the customer's objection is real. To determine this, you ask four key questions. The questions must be asked in the order shown. You may end up vaporizing the objection with question 1, because the customer will respond with something absurd, allowing you to move off the topic of price until the time is right.

▶ Question 1: "Compared with what?" Or, "Can you explain that?" Oftentimes, however, the customer says something silly, like, "My grandfather told me to expect a price of $_____ ." Or "I have a bid from eighty-eight years ago, and the price was much lower." Or "I have a competitive bid from another company for the exact same offering as you." Further questioning reveals that the bid is not even close to being competitive. If the customer's response is indeed sound, then you have two options: You can attempt to sell your value by highlighting your lower TCO or higher ROI, or you can move on to Question 2.

▶ Question 2: "Are you ready to make your final decision now?" Unless the customer is ready to buy now — not four months from now — there should be no negotiations about price. If the customer is set to buy now, continue with Question 3.

- ▶ Question 3: "Removing the initial investment from the decision just for the moment, are you 110% convinced that we offer the right solution and that there are absolutely no other issues to be addressed?" (Notice that you should use the more graceful term *initial investment* instead of *price*.) You do *not* want to be negotiating price at the same time that you're negotiating delivery and installation schedules. Don't muddy the price waters with other issues. If there are no outstanding issues, continue with Question 4.

- ▶ Question 4: "Please share with me what the price delta is so that I can make a sound case to my management, and I'll do my very best to narrow the gap."

Your goal is to get price off the table unless the customer is actually set to buy now and there are absolutely no other outstanding issues. Said another way, negotiate price as a final issue: (a) when the customer has realistic expectations; (b) when the customer is set to buy now, not later; (c) when the customer is convinced that your solution meets her needs; and (d) when you have an idea of where *you* need your price to be. Once a superstar understands where the price needs to be, she never lowers the price but tries to provide increased value in lieu of a lower price.

Four Key Questions to Ask in Response to Price Objections

1 "Compared with what?" Or, "Can you explain that?"

2 "Are you ready to make your final decision now?"

3 "Are you 110% convinced that we offer the right solution and there are absolutely no other issues to be addressed?"

4 "Please share with me what the price delta is so that I can make a sound case to my management."

UNDERSTAND YOUR CONTRIBUTION MARGIN — DON'T DROP PRICE

As a superstar you should *never* drop the price; instead, offer additional products or services that equal or exceed the requested discount. The impact of a price drop on your net income would be substantial, whereas providing a product or service decreases your net income only by the wholesale cost (not the retail cost) of that extra product or service. When choosing which products or services to offer in a negotiation, choose those with high contribution margins, such as software, maintenance, and warranty.

GIVE SLOWLY AND RELUCTANTLY

During final negotiations, whenever you offer a price concession, do not make major reductions. Any major shift in price or position signals to customers that much greater concessions could be had for the asking. And believe me, they will ask.

During my final negotiations for a software solution at one of the largest food companies in the world, the customer asked my manager and me for a price concession on our $18 million quotation. When my manager responded with a price of $8 million, I almost died. A drop of $10 million in the selling price after I had fought hard for more than a year to sell the value of our offering! What happened here? I made a huge mistake in not preparing my manager more thoroughly with a Trade Matrix. As a consequence, we lost credibility in the eyes of our customer. After all, what was the value of our offering if we could reduce the price by $10 million in three seconds? Who was to blame for the errors? I was, of course. If I had been a sales superstar, I would have reviewed and rehearsed our pricing strategy to ensure there were no surprises.

BEWARE OF CHIP

Have you met "Chip" during your negotiations? Chip is an expert at piecemeal negotiations. Chip is the purchasing director who continues to chip away at your negotiations, asking for one thing at a time. He holds his negotiation demands close to his vest and releases them one by one. Maybe it's "Oh, I forgot, I need more warranty," or "I'm assuming that you will be including five years of accessories and supplies?" This has the psychological effect of wearing the sales rep down. She never knows when the negotiations have reached a conclusion; she never knows what's coming next. It puts the buyer in a much more powerful position.

To handle Chip, a superstar will insist that Chip put all his issues onto the table *before* addressing any of them. That way, the superstar can assess what's at stake and fashion an offer that balances the totality of Chip's requests with what the superstar is able to concede. If Chip presses, an effective reply is, "I may be able to ask my manager to make some small concessions, but until I resolve all of your outstanding issues I will be forced to say no to each of your requests."

I'M JUST A CAVEMAN

Avoid flaunting your superstar status during the negotiations. If you let slip the fact that you are a veteran negotiator who has been through this a million times, you will feel a brick wall rising up between you and the customer. I like to say, at least in my head, "I'm just a caveman." Present yourself as a non-expert (*only* with regard to the negotiation process, *not* to your product or service expertise). You will be astonished at how much the customer wants to help you. The negotiation instantly takes on a win-win feel when the customer does not feel vulnerable. Remind him that you are in this process together, working toward a mutually beneficial solution. Assure him that you will advocate for the best solution your company can offer.

EVERY OFFER MUST HAVE AN EXPIRATION DATE

It would be a major mistake to make an offer to your customer and let her "think about it" for an indefinite amount of time. Each offer must have a mutually agreed upon expiration date committed to paper.

SEND A NEGOTIATION FOLLOW-UP LETTER

The terms of the agreement and the agreed upon expiration date must be committed to writing in the negotiation follow-up letter. Have you ever heard this complaint from sales reps? "My customer let the expiration date pass but still expects the same deal!" The fix for this problem is simple. You anticipate its occurrence and announce to the customer certain quid pro quo consequences: A price increase goes into effect as soon as the expiration date passes.

Let's say that you convince the customer to provide a purchase order on or before December 31 as a condition of your concessions. The moment that you agree to these concessions you also explain that your company is depending on this business and that the concessions are dependent upon your receiving a contingency-free purchase order on or before December 31. If, for any reason, you do not receive the purchase order by that date, the price increases from X dollars to Y dollars.

You may be in a position to explain, "Our manufacturing floor has been loaded based on our agreement. With any change, we would be facing high inventory-carrying costs. As a result, I need to make our commitment terms clear." Or you might say, "Our special offer has been provided because your business is critical to our corporation's meeting its financial targets for this quarter."

Secret Weapon 31 is the negotiation follow-up letter that I typically use. Does this letter stop the customer from calling to say he will not have the purchase order by the agreed upon date? No, but it makes it very hard for him to do so. If he does call to delay, you are in the driver's seat; you can decide exactly how you want to handle the situation. The customer might say, "It was unavoidable. We tried as hard as we could. I'm sure you aren't really to raise the price on us, right?" You can respond a number of ways:

- ▶ Review with the customer the letter containing the agreed upon terms and remind him how much the delay will damage his company — for instance, "A two-week delay in signing the purchase order will cost you $50,000 in lost revenue, because the installation will also be delayed."

SECRET WEAPON 31

Negotiation Follow-up Letter

Lee Gannon
Senior Vice President
ABC Corporation
18 Thorndike Road
Wakefield, MA 01880

Dear Lee:

This is a follow-up to our recent discussion regarding your new Imaging System project. Adams & Associates agrees to lower our price for the Imaging System to **$1.5M.**

As part of this price concession, ABC Corporation has agreed to the following:

▶ Contingency-free purchase order to be received on or before August 3, 2008.

▶ Signed financing documents on or before August 10, 2008.

▶ Delivery and installation of the equipment on or before September 8, 2008.

▶ The special pricing and terms of this agreement are to be held in the strictest confidence.

We also agree that the price becomes $1.7M if the contingency-free purchase order is not received on or before August 3, 2008.

Thank you for working with us to construct an understanding that allows us to deliver an incredible overall deal to ABC Corporation. We are excited about the opportunity and appreciate your business.

Sincerely,

Ben

Benjamin Edwards
cell 630-555-1212

▶ Use the higher authority close. Tell the customer you will check with your manager before responding to the request to keep the price the same.

▶ Would you stand hard on the price increase outlined in your negotiation follow-up letter? Maybe, but I believe the more prudent move for a superstar interested in nurturing a long-term relationship with her customer is to not increase the price. I would, however, use quid pro quo to get something of value from the customer, such as a commitment for future business, the purchase of additional options, an opportunity to meet with senior customer executives, financing, the purchase of additional support and maintenance, or a customer testimonial. "I understand the difficulties you are having. I wonder if you would be willing to provide certain concessions to offset the difficulties the delay will cause us?"

The fifteen negotiation best practices (above) put you in the position where closing is the next natural step.

▶ Step 5 — Gaining Commitment ◀

True or false: Closing occurs only at the end of the sale. This is false. Superstars know that closing, or gaining commitment, occurs throughout the entire buying process. The definition of closing, for me, is helping people make decisions that are good for them. It is not talking people into buying something they don't need or want. Closing begins the very first time you contact your customer. Gaining commitment for an appointment, receiving permission to document the customer's buying process, gaining access to the CxO – these are all closes.

Ten Consultative Closes

There are many books on the topic of closing. Most closes are too manipulative to be used by a superstar sales rep. The following can be used professionally without jeopardizing your credibility.

▶ *Sharp Angle (If/Then) Close.* This is the standard quid pro quo close used by a superstar whenever the customer asks for something. Be careful to round off the sharp corners on your response so the customer is not turned off by a harsh give-get transaction.

▶ *Puppy Dog Close.* The puppy dog close works great if it is possible for your customers to test-drive your solution – for instance, if you have the ability to upgrade products with software. If you were a dog breeder you would sell a lot of puppies if you allowed families to try out a puppy for a week. What are the chances of the parents returning a puppy after the kids have bonded with their new friend? Similarly, once a customer has tried out your solution and discovered how well it relieves his pain, it is very difficult to return the solution and go back to his old ways.

▶ *Summary Close.* In this simple close, you summarize what you have agreed upon or reviewed during a meeting, and then suggest the logical next steps.

▶ *Report Card Close.* After a presentation, solution demonstration, equipment site visit, or any other major event for which you have put in a great deal of time and effort to meet the customer's specific requirements (in other words, any time you have deployed your personal and corporate scarce resources), you are owed an evaluation of your efforts by the customer. I like to ask for a report card on my efforts — using a scale of 1 (worst) to 10 (best), or grades from A (best) to F (worst). I then follow up with a simple question close (see below) as to how I could improve. You might be surprised at what you can uncover by asking for a frank appraisal of your performance. I've learned a lot about my own sales competencies.

Amazingly, sometimes customers also offer information on how your competitors performed. When I was trying to sell a software solution to a customer, I was in last place. But after a presentation and demonstration with my applications engineer, we made progress. When I asked for my report card, the customer said that, in comparison with our solution, the solution of our biggest competitor performed "like a car without windows or doors." His comment helped us regain our enthusiasm. Over time, we overcame the customer's other objections and eventually won the deal.

▶ *Assumptive Close.* During an assumptive close, you take action as if the customer has asked you to do so. "I'll be back next week at the same time to review the revised paperwork with you." Among the closes presented here, this is the most risky, because you run the risk of the customer balking at the requested steps — and damaging your credibility. Before using an assumptive close you should feel fairly certain that the customer will agree to the steps you are suggesting.

▶ *Alternate Choice Close.* In an alternative choice close you simply provide options to the customer, all of which are acceptable to you. "Would next Thursday or Friday work better for your calendar?"

▶ *Higher Authority Close.* A good time to use the higher authority close is whenever a customer makes a major demand. Perhaps the customer says, "I really need you to lower your financing rate," or "Your maintenance costs are way out of line." First, you let the customer know that as a quid pro quo you'll need some more information. For instance, if the objection has to do with price, you would need to know whether the customer's objection is real; whether the customer is ready to buy; whether absolutely no other issues are preventing her from investing in your solution; and the price delta needed to win the deal. Then you let the customer know that any major concession will require your manager's approval. You also make use of this close in response to price-related customer objections (see Handle the Price Objection, page 138).

▶ *Reduce It to the Ridiculous Close.* This close can help minimize a price delta. Let's say the customer tells you that your price is $60,000 too high. You reframe that $60,000 by using a different unit of measure. "Our solution is fairly priced. Over a five-year period that difference is only $33 per day. Wouldn't you pay $33 for the assurance that you've bought the right solution?"

▶ *Similar Situation Close.* This is the best close to use with top executives. I use it when setting up appointments at the senior levels of an organization. "We have been very successful at addressing this same issue for many other companies. I believe we may be able to assist you." (See Secret Weapon 16 – Power Letter on page 86.)

▶ *Simple Question Close.* It doesn't get much more straightforward than this. You say, "What do you suggest we do to earn your business?"

Battling Cognitive Dissonance

Just as people buy for emotional, not rational, reasons, they sometimes back out of deals for emotional, not rational, reasons. The customer bought the product or service because he wanted to avoid pain or solve a problem. Sometimes, after the sale, he receives new information that makes him doubt whether he made the right decision. This inconsistency between what he originally thought ("This is a great deal") and what he thinks now ("I'm not so sure this is the best deal") creates discomfort. This discomfort pushes the customer to action – either canceling the deal or adjusting his thinking so he can once again settle on the original belief ("This truly is a great deal").

Cognitive dissonance, first proposed by the psychologist Leon Festinger in 1956, describes the tendency of human beings to seek consistency among their beliefs and opinions and their discomfort with any inconsistency – that is, dissonance. In economics this phenomenon is called buyer's remorse. After people make a major purchase they begin to doubt themselves. Let's say a customer buys a new shop vac based on her sister-in-law's recommendation and what the salesperson in the store told her about the product. The day after deciding on the shop vac she reads *Consumer Reports* and finds out that another brand of shop vac has higher ratings. This puts her in a conflicted state of mind; she regrets buying the shop vac because it was the "wrong" one. Psychologically, she wants to attain psychological consonance – that is, a balance between these competing opinions.

The customer can eliminate the contradiction by adding a third piece of information – by saying to herself, "Although it's true that *Consumer Reports* gave the Widgetizer shop vac higher ratings, the only store that sells those is in the next county, and the brand I bought can be serviced two blocks away." The contradiction is resolved; the dissonance has changed to consonance; the buyer's remorse melts away.

The higher the risk involved in the purchase, the more likely the buyer will feel some remorse. Buying a $200 shop vac involves relatively little risk; buying multimillion-dollar technology or software for a fast-expanding business with a cash flow problem is high risk indeed.

The superstar knows that the moment the customer comes close to making a decision or finalizing a purchase is a very delicate time in the sales process, one that could even lead to the customer's changing vendors at the last minute. Such negative decisions can be avoided – or reversed, if they do occur – by careful attention on the part of the sales rep:

▶ Remind the customer, if necessary, about the extensive process he went through to select your solution. Remind him of the concessions you made – not to make him feel guilty or to play the role of the victim but to reinforce the belief that he got a good deal and made the right decision. Do anything you can to convince the customer that you will be there with him for the long haul.

▶ Attend the birth of your baby. Be on-site the first few days after the decision is made and on the days when your solution is delivered, installed, and first used. Customers don't want you to dine and dash – that is, grab their money and disappear.

▶ Throw a party when the solution is first ready for use. I sometimes bring in a sheet cake decorated with the customer's logo and a photo of the product.

- ▶ Get in the habit of maintaining constant contact with your customers. The last thing you want is the customer off by herself, doubting the deal she made – and perhaps talking with your competitors. Send win letters (Secret Weapon 32) and schedule Exceeding Expectations Meetings. Each is described below.

Win Letter

Immediately send a win letter **(Secret Weapon 32)** after a win. The timing of the letter is extremely important. You should send it as soon as you receive word from the decision maker that she has formally decided on your solution. Do *not* wait for the final purchase order. If you do, you may never get the opportunity to send it. A win letter has three purposes:

First, it serves to battle cognitive dissonance, or buyer's remorse. After making a major decision it is human nature to doubt the decision. The superstar delivers this letter to stifle any second thoughts that might arise in the mind of the decision maker by reminding him of all the good reasons he made the choice he made.

Second, a win letter helps to defend against the all-out assault sure to come from your competitors once they hear that they will lose this opportunity. During this time the competition will try almost anything to convince the customer to change his mind. Dramatic price drops; flying in the CEO from Europe; free accessories; use it for one year free, and then pay; free installation; a five-year warranty – you name it, I've seen it! Since a final purchase order could take days or months to process, in the mind of your customer the letter provides closure to the process and may help terminate the competitor relationships. Sending the letter solidifies the finality of the customer's choice to buy from you. It is worded in such a way that your customer believes that vendor selection is complete, and there is no reason to continue discussion with other vendors.

Third, the win letter makes it clear you are a superstar. It includes a strong commitment from you not to dine and dash or disengage from the customer now that the sale is made.

Exceeding Expectations Meeting

When is an order an order? An order is not an order just because the customer gives you a verbal commitment or has signed a contract. An order is not even an order when the money is in the bank. In the mind of the superstar, an order is an order only when the customer is completely satisfied, she actively recommends your solution to her colleagues, and she continues to buy from your company.

SECRET WEAPON 32

Win Letter

Lee Gannon
Senior Vice President
ABC Corporation
18 Thorndike Road
Wakefield, MA 01880

Dear Lee:

We have just received the great news that you have committed to investing in Adams & Associates' Imaging System. ABC Corporation joins a long list of prestigious, well-respected healthcare organizations that have chosen to install this system. Dr. Aidan Farrow of the Mundelein Clinic called the Imaging System "the standard all others are trying to achieve."

As you know, we have worked very hard to earn your business over the past eight months. But I firmly believe that the real work begins now. I will be working overtime to ensure that we exceed your expectations and meet all our commitments to you.

Step one in reaching that goal is to set up our Exceeding Expectations Meeting, which will kick off the planning for the site preparation, delivery, installation, and applications training. You will be hearing from me soon regarding possible meeting dates.

Once again, thank you very much for your business.

Sincerely,

Ben

Benjamin Edwards
cell 630-555-1212

cc: Alice Murphy, MD

After the contract is signed you might say to yourself, "Congratulations! I won!" And then you think, "Now what?" Well, you have already managed cognitive dissonance with your win letter. The next step is to set up an Exceeding Expectations Meeting, which has several purposes. The meeting establishes you as the go-to person in this deal – as the key person the customer trusts. Why do you care? Because you want all of this customer's future business, not just the current deal, and you want the customer to believe very strongly that she has made the right decision.

> ★ SUPERSTAR SECRET ★
>
> **An order is an order only after you have a satisfied customer who actively recommends your solution to others – *and* becomes a repeat customer.**

The point of the meeting is to make sure you and the customer jointly understand what happens next. You review the time lines for delivery, site preparation, and installation. Take ownership of these deadlines; your customer's trust in you depends on them. At the meeting it is crucial that you discuss payment terms. You also discuss upgrade possibilities, service, training, and options. In addition, you review your customer's definition of the criteria that will make this project a success. You take great notes and revisit your performance against these criteria during step 7, the final feedback stage.

At the meeting, write your home phone number on the back of your business card, hand it to your customer, and invite him to call you if he ever has any problems. This extra courtesy demonstrates your concern for your customer's success and can help secure future business.

Close Plan Letter

Let's say the customer gives you verbal agreement to purchase your product. Even with that in place, events can occur that could jeopardize your sale. A close plan letter (**Secret Weapon 33**) is an effective way to manage the unpredictability of this stage of the game. It outlines the steps necessary to take the customer from her verbal commitment to the issuing of a formal purchase order and down payment. The superstar uses the letter to micromanage the steps to complete the process, limit any surprises, and hasten the sale.

Can the win letter and close plan letter be combined into one document? *No.* The win letter and the close plan letter have different purposes. The win letter's purpose is to battle cognitive dissonance and keep competitors at bay; the close plan letter's purpose is to prevent surprises in the run-up to the final purchase order.

SECRET WEAPON 33

Close Plan Letter

Ann Hamilton
Senior Vice President
SISU Corporation
4143 Pine Street
San Francisco, CA 94104

Dear Ann:

Thank you for meeting with me today to discuss the Upgrade Project.

This note serves as a summary of the action items needed to finalize the paperwork and approvals by January 10. To process the order, we will need the following:

Action Item	Owner	Completion Date	Comment
Departmental approval			
Legal approval			
Board approval			
Signed contractual quotation (AA-ABC08B)	Amy Redmond		
Signed purchase order referencing the quotation number (AA-ABC08B) and the total dollar amount ($1.5M)	Amy Redmond		
Signed trade-in addendum permitting us to remove the existing system	Amy Redmond		
Signed financing documents	Amy Redmond		

I will call Eleanor on Friday to set up an early December status review meeting.

Sincerely,

Ben

Benjamin Edwards
cell 630-555-1212

Loss Letter

Obviously, if you've won the contract you don't send a loss letter (**Secret Weapon 34**). I mention loss letters here, along with win letters and close plan letters, because you should be sending letters at every stage of the selling process. When an average sales rep loses a sale, she gives a silent harrumph, closes the file, and walks away. Many reps contact the customer and whine like little babies. I'm amazed at how many reps act this way. All this does is confirm in the customer's mind that he made the right decision to work with someone else. A superstar sales rep, on the other hand, knows all about cognitive dissonance and knows that the customer is buying continually, and therefore stays in touch to nurture that long-term relationship. He sends a loss letter and perhaps follows up with a phone call with wishes of good luck and a request for feedback on how he could improve in the future.

And who knows? Yes, the customer picked another vendor, but perhaps your competitor will allow cognitive dissonance to set in – or perhaps she will even cause it. Some vendors don't keep their promises; they dine and dash. Business catastrophes might occur, and the customer may decide to jump to another vendor. If you've kept the lines of communication open, that other vendor might well be you. A loss letter, which invites the continuance of the relationship even after the loss of the sale, is good business.

I have personally seen where this approach has paid off handsomely. I sent a customer a loss letter after working with him for several months on a very large X-ray system. The customer chose a competitor for a large diagnostic imaging center project only to cancel the order before it was delivered. He decided to work with me without talking to any of the other competitors. He said the primary reason for this turnaround was the poor follow-up he had received from my competitor and the way that I had gained his trust throughout the entire buying process.

These so-called small steps – loss letters, win letters, close plan letters, and Exceeding Expectations Meetings – cost you little more than a few minutes of your time but can reap huge payoffs. Make them second nature. They help you, as a superstar, D^3 – develop, document, and drive the customer's buying process.

▶ Step 6 — Implementing the Solution ◀

Average reps grab the order and are never seen again by the customer. Superstars don't dine and dash. Your job is to stay in the loop and ensure that all the commitments you made have been met or exceeded. Putting together a post-installation reception at the customer organization will also differentiate you as a superstar.

▶ Step 7 — Gathering Feedback ◀

As we discussed early on, the goal of a superstar is to establish long-term relationships with customers — relationships that last years and, we hope, result in numerous sales. In step 7 you revisit both your performance on this project and the customer's expectations that were gathered in the Exceeding Expectations Meeting, when you asked your customer to provide her criteria for project success. A final meeting is held with the customer to review your performance against these criteria. This provides further evidence of your willingness to go above and beyond to ensure your customer's success and continue to earn her trust in you.

SECRET WEAPON 34

Loss Letter

Melinda Gatlin
Vice President
AEM Company
2 Huntington Road
Denver, Colorado 80215

Dear Melinda:

Over the past several months I have been working closely with your staff to satisfy your System Upgrade needs. Last week I was informed of your decision to work with another vendor for this project.

Though naturally I am disappointed that AEM Company has not selected Adams & Associates, I would like to extend my sincere appreciation for the opportunity to have presented our offering.

I wish you the best of luck as you begin the challenging and rewarding process of expanding your services.

Please contact me at any time if my team or I can be of assistance to you during the System Upgrade design, installation, and training processes.

Sincerely,

Ben

Benjamin Edwards
cell 630-555-1212

CHAPTER FIVE

PUTTING IT ALL TOGETHER

We've covered a lot of territory together. Let's circle back to where we started – your mission as a sales superstar. Your job is not to sell but to consult, thereby helping your customers invest in the appropriate product or solution. By developing, documenting, and driving (D^3) the customer's buying process, you guide customers down a mutually agreed upon pathway toward the sale.

Selling like a superstar is good for the psyche. Although you work hard, you are able to stay calm, because you have a plan for most contingencies. You are always thinking ahead. Once you practice these steps and integrate the processes, you begin to imagine various scenarios and what strategy you would employ, in the smallest detail. You're not glib, and you don't have an answer for everything, but you understand the patterns in the customer interactions. You sleep well at night because you maintain your integrity, genuinely serving customers. Plus, of course, you are likely to be much more successful, which brings its own peace of mind.

In chapter 3 we described the customer's buying process, and in chapter 4 we described the superstar selling process. It's time now to put them together – to look at how the superstar rep takes care of the customer's buying process needs and her own selling process needs simultaneously, using which tool when. When you merge these two processes, you achieve a matchless meeting of the minds when the customer's buying process and your sales process are in synch.

Applying the Tools

	Customer Buying Process	Superstar Selling Process	Secret Weapons and Key Concepts
1	Develop the corporate strategic plan	Identify opportunities	▶ Trust Triangle ▶ Secret Weapon 3: New Account Introduction Letter ▶ Secret Weapon 15: Value Proposition Worksheet ▶ Prospecting Machine ▶ Secret Weapon 16: Power Letter ▶ Secret Weapon 17: Power Phone Script ▶ Secret Weapon 18: Territory Attack Plan
2	Uncover needs and develop the business case	Qualify prospects	▶ Trust Triangle ▶ D^3 — Develop, document, and drive the customer's buying process ▶ Compelling event ▶ Compelling event time line ▶ Secret Weapon 4: Simple Process Letter ▶ Secret Weapon 5: Buying Process: Table Format ▶ Secret Weapon 6: Buying Process: Time Line Format ▶ Secret Weapon 7: Buying Process: Calendar Format ▶ Secret Weapon 8: Buying Process: Column Format ▶ Secret Weapon 9: Buying Process: Gantt Chart Format ▶ Secret Weapon 14: Mutual Memo of Understanding ▶ COW Questioning Technique ▶ Secret Weapon 19: BMPCC Account Qualification Template ▶ Secret Weapon 20: Power Quid Pro Quo Letter ▶ Secret Weapon 21: Response to Surprise Proposal Request

Applying the Tools (continued)

	Customer Buying Process	Superstar Selling Process	Secret Weapons and Key Concepts
3	Assess potential solutions	Select the strategy	▸ Trust Triangle ▸ Secret Weapon 1: Request for Vendor References ▸ Secret Weapon 2: Vendor Report Card ▸ My field! My rules! My time! My game! ▸ Secret Weapon 22: Strategic Plan ▸ Eight Major Account Strategies ▸ Secret Weapon 23: Customer Decision Matrix ▸ Secret Weapon 24: Disengage Letter ▸ Secret Weapon 25: Budgetary Pricing Letter ▸ Secret Weapon 26: Budgetary Pricing Proposal
4	Evaluate vendors	Provide proof and justification	▸ Trust Triangle ▸ Secret Weapon 10: Presentation Protocol Letter ▸ Secret Weapon 11: Presentation Report Card ▸ Secret Weapon 12: Request for Proposal Cover Letter ▸ Secret Weapon 13: Request for Proposal Excerpt ▸ Secret Weapon 27: Selling Value Matrix ▸ Secret Weapon 28: Value-Added Matrix ▸ Secret Weapon 29: Objection Vaporizer ▸ Secret Weapon 30: Trade Matrix
5	Finalize vendor selection	Gain commitment	▸ Trust Triangle ▸ Negotiation Best Practices ▸ Secret Weapon 31: Negotiation Follow-up Letter ▸ Ten Consultative Closes ▸ Secret Weapon 32: Win Letter ▸ Secret Weapon 33: Close Plan Letter ▸ Secret Weapon 34: Loss Letter ▸ Exceeding Expectations Meeting
6	Implement the solution		▸ Trust Triangle ▸ Exceeding Expectations Meeting
7	Gather feedback		▸ Trust Triangle ▸ Customer Satisfaction Report

Let's walk through a hypothetical sale from start to finish, discussing the tools you would use at each step along the way, using Superstar Ben Edwards as our example.

► Case Study ◄

Ben is a sales rep for Adams & Associates, a manufacturer of CT scanners. Ben has done his homework; he's well familiar with his company's value proposition (Secret Weapon 15) and the concepts of the Trust Triangle. In collaboration with his sales manager, Joe Feider, Ben has put together a Territory Attack Plan (Secret Weapon 18), setting goals for the year. He's in the habit of calling on the accounts in his territory, leaving behind his business card as a footprint and noting whose cars are parked in the account's parking lots.

During step 1 of the superstar selling process, prospecting, Ben revs up his Prospecting Machine and identifies ten prospects. He has discovered that one prospect in his territory, Acme Hospital, has lost ground to competing hospitals in the same city, because Acme's CT scanners and imaging center can handle only a limited number of patients, though demand for the service is high, based on the demographics of the area.

Ben takes bits and pieces of Adams & Associates' value proposition to create a customized Power Letter (Secret Weapon 16) to Lucy, a Senior Vice President of Acme Hospital, highlighting the challenge the hospital is facing, touting the ROI of his newest scanner, and quoting a satisfied customer as a reference.

He follows up the letter with a phone call to SVP Lucy, using the Power Phone Script (Secret Weapon 17). He sets up an appointment to meet with her. (If Acme Hospital was an existing customer of Adams & Associates, and Ben was the new rep, Ben's boss, Joe, would first send a New Account Introduction Letter [Secret Weapon 3] to Lucy, introducing Ben. Ben would then follow up with a phone call to set up an appointment.)

During step 2 of the sales process, qualification, Ben meets with Lucy to discuss her hospital's needs. At this stage he uses both the COW questioning technique along with the BMPCC account qualification template. Through COW questioning he learns about Lucy's *current* situation, her *optimal* situation, and how the successful completion of her project would be a *win* for her hospital and herself. He does not pull out brochures or discuss the dimensions of the scanner. He asks about her concerns and finds out what's at stake for her and her hospital. He discovers that although a new CT scanner is part of the hospital's corporate strategic plan, Lucy has never had the responsibility of purchasing one.

Thanks to Ben's adept use of the BMPCC account qualification criteria early in the buying process (Secret Weapon 19), he realizes that SVP Lucy is not the only decision maker in this deal. Margaret, the CFO, will have the final say. From his questioning strategy Ben learns that the due date (compelling event) for the purchase is December 31, to coincide with the renovation of one wing of the hospital.

Since Ben knows he is still on the left-hand slope of the Trust Triangle, he wouldn't dream of rushing toward a sale or unload data about his product's facts and features. Instead, he builds trust by establishing his credibility, showing concern, and displaying sufficient competence.

Using the concepts of D^3, he begins to develop, document, and drive Lucy's buying process, explaining that he is in the business of preventing headaches for her, *whether she decides to buy from him or not*. He shares success stories of other hospitals he has helped, and offers tools that can guide her through every step of the process.

He shows her appropriate Request for Vendor References (Secret Weapon 1) and Vendor Report Card (Secret Weapon 2) as examples of how other customers have handled such a purchase. He explains that his goal is the success of her project, and he offers himself as her unpaid advisor through it all.

Lucy seems a bit resistant to Ben's help and simply wants to jump ahead to talking about the dollars. When Lucy requests a formal pricing quotation Ben explains that getting random prices from several vendors would not be in *her* best interests right now – first, he needs to help her figure out what would meet her needs. Ben uses this opportunity to help Lucy understand the many headaches that will occur if he and other vendors begin to provide pricing now. He gives her several examples of the chaos that will occur without a generic bid specification that the vendors can use to price their offerings. In so doing he positions himself as a consultant who can assist Lucy at the appropriate time with generic proposal specifications (Secret Weapon 12: Request for Proposal Cover Letter and Secret Weapon 13: Request for Proposal Excerpt).

Lucy sounds dubious. "I don't get it," she says. "Why would you do this?" Ben replies, "Because I've found that, in the long run, helping my customers is good business. Sometimes I get the sale, sometimes I don't. Either way, I have the satisfaction of knowing I've helped the customer. And I sleep well at night."

After his meeting with Lucy, Ben sends her a Simple Process Letter (Secret Weapon 4), outlining next steps. He also sends a Mutual Memo of Understanding (Secret Weapon 14).

Ben privately summarizes the information he gathers from these conversations on a BMPCC Account Qualification Template (Secret Weapon 19), which he keeps updated throughout the selling process.

When Lucy tries to get Ben to bid on the project prematurely, he sends her a Power Quid Pro Quo Letter (Secret Weapon 20), explaining that he is happy to provide budgetary pricing information but would also request the opportunity to make a presentation to the CFO. He carefully leverages her request to get what he needs, without saying so in so many words. Ben solicits Lucy's assistance in arranging a meeting with CFO Margaret.

When meeting with Margaret, Ben starts over, climbing the Trust Triangle again. In the course of their discussions, she reveals that the hospital is indeed serious about the purchase and has sufficient budget to move forward.

CFO Margaret is overloaded with responsibilities and is happy to have Ben's help. Ben encourages her to contact other hospitals to gather information on the solutions the hospital is considering. Ben indicates that he will work closely with Lucy to drive this project to a successful completion by the compelling event. Ben removes any doubt or anxiety Margaret may have when he displays his preparation and professionalism by sharing with her a customized Acme Hospital Buying Process (Secret Weapons 5 through 9), which ensures the project's completion by December 31 (compelling event). This confirms in Margaret's and Lucy's minds that Ben is a true superstar and that he can be trusted with a high-risk, big-ticket project like this one.

Throughout the whole sales process, Ben makes sure that the solution SVP Lucy and the CFO Margaret are buying is in the hospital's best interests – even if it means not buying from him. He refuses to sell the customers something that will not serve them well.

During step 3, strategy selection, Ben assesses Acme Hospital's needs, decision criteria rack and stack, the CFO's personal style, and the competitors on the scene. He discovers that initial cost is *currently* the CFO's number one buying criteria. He creates an in-house Customer Decision Matrix (Secret Weapon 23) to get a sense of where his solution stands relative to the competition. Ben sees that if he goes head-to-head on price, he is likely to lose. Since he is definitely not the low-cost provider, but his company does offer the best service, he chooses as his strategy Change the Game – New Game, with the goal of elevating system performance and quality of service to the top of the CFO's buying criteria (see table of Eight Major Account Strategies, page 106). He puts together a Strategic Plan (Secret Weapon 22) that includes his strategy and specific tactics.

CFO Margaret, like SVP Lucy, requests some ballpark numbers to see if the budget for the project is adequate. Ben provides a Budgetary Pricing Letter and Proposal (Secret Weapons 25 and 26) to reassure the CFO.

During stage 4, proof and justification, Ben helps Lucy set up vendor presentations by providing the template for a Presentation Protocol Letter (Secret Weapon 10). He helps Lucy structure the evaluation of these presentations with a Presentation Report Card (Secret Weapon 11). He hands this to Lucy saying, "Here's a tool to help you evaluate what you hear." Ben makes sure his unfair advantages – a terrific service record and performance capabilities – are among the criteria on the report card. Following the philosophy of My Field, My Time, My Game, My Rules, Ben makes sure that he presents last, in a pleasant, appropriate environment, not a stuffy basement conference room. After the presentations CFO Margaret is ready to ask for quotes from three of the presenters, including Ben. Ben works with Lucy on the generic bid specifications by starting with a Request for Proposal template (Secret Weapons 12 and 13). Ben continues to give Margaret periodic updates on the progress of the project.

Ben puts together an in-house Selling Value Matrix (Secret Weapon 27) to clarify for himself his solution's unfair advantage and why, specifically, a customer should be willing to pay more because of it. He assists SVP Lucy in preparing a Value-Added Matrix (Secret Weapon 28) for CFO Margaret, outlining in simple black and white the bottom-line, hard-dollar advantage of his solution. He never ruins the trust Lucy and Margaret have placed in him by slanting the document only in his favor. He is open and truthful throughout the entire process.

When Margaret raises objections, Ben is thrilled, because the objections indicate interest. Ben uses the seven Vaporizing Objections steps on page 129. He skillfully addresses the objections raised by Margaret and Lucy. He uses the word *trade-offs* (page 78) when discussing the major differences between his solution and those offered by other vendors.

Based on his knowledge of the customer, Ben chooses a Simple Question Close (page 145). He asks Margaret, "What do you suggest we do to earn your business?" CFO Margaret says that she concerned about the high cost of Ben's quote. Ben recognizes this as a major buying signal but does *not* cave on price. He skillfully makes use of the four key questions (see Handle the Price Objection, page 138) to ask when faced with any price-related issue.

Margaret: "Your price is a bit steep."

Ben: "Oh… Compared with what?"

Margaret (smiling): "The apples-to-apples competitive proposals that were provided in response to the generic bid specifications that you helped us with."

Ben: "Are you set to invest now?"

Margaret: "Yes, we're all set to go to the board by Friday."

Ben: "OK, removing price from the table for just a second, are you 110% convinced we're the correct investment for Acme and that there are absolutely no other issues?"

Margaret: "Yes, I think so."

Ben realizes that "I think so" is not acceptable, so he closes again.

Ben: "Are you sure that you have no other concerns — legal, delivery, installation, service and support costs?"

Margaret: "Well, yes… Your support costs are a bit high."

Ben: "Other than the service and support costs and equipment cost, is everything 110% acceptable?"

Margaret (finally relenting): "Yes."

Ben moves to the last question.

Ben: "Share with me your target price for the equipment and service, and I'll do my best to work with my manager to narrow the gap." (See Higher Authority Close, page 145.)

Margaret suggests a face-to-face meeting with Ben's manager, Joe, and Ben agrees (see The Lone Ranger Is Dead, page 137).

Ben has gained commitment (step 5 in the Superstar Selling Process) and correctly prepared the customer for a negotiation meeting. Now he must prepare Joe. Ben internally prepares a Trade Matrix (Secret Weapon 30) and reviews it with Joe to help them clarify the issues during the negotiations. He is now on the right side of the Trust Triangle, sliding smoothly toward the sale. But he needs to be careful. Anything can happen. Ben pays attention and assumes nothing.

When Ben and Joe meet with Margaret, Joe correctly responds to Margaret's request for a lower price by not lowering price but by providing increased value. He knows *never* to lower price (see Negotiation Best Practices, page 135). Joe saves contribution margin by providing a series of incentives that, together with the rest of the package, equate to a value that Margaret finds irresistible. Joe reduces the financing rate, increases the warranty, and includes an additional software package at no additional charge. The deal is made!

After whooping to his manager in the parking lot, Ben immediately sends the key players three letters. He sends a Negotiation Follow-up Letter (Secret Weapon 31) to ensure that Margaret meets her commitment to provide the purchase order on the date they all agreed upon. He sends a Win Letter (Secret Weapon 32) to battle buyer's remorse and defend against the sure-to-come all-out assault of his competitors. Finally, he sends a Close Plan Letter (Secret Weapon 33) to outline the steps needed to finalize the approvals and to prevent surprises.

Ben calls Margaret a few days later and senses some concern about whether she made the right choice. Ben helps her justify her choice by providing additional facts and figures that support her decision. He gives Margaret additional proof to share with her superiors — the hospital board. Ben behaves impeccably during every interaction.

During step 6, implementation, Ben oversees every detail of the installation or implementation of the solution and sets up an Exceeding Expectations Meeting. During this meeting he reviews the delivery, site preparation, implementation, and installation. In addition, he reviews the criteria by which Margaret will consider this project a success. Ben takes great notes and revisits his performance and his company's performance against these criteria after the completion of the project.

Finally, at the end of the project, Ben hosts a party in the hospital's imaging center to celebrate the project's roaring success.

After the system has been up and running for several weeks, Ben meets again with the decision team to get open, honest feedback on how he and his company performed against the success criteria provided during the Exceeding Expectations Meeting. This meeting cements the very long and mutually beneficial relationship that Ben and Acme Hospital will have for many years to come.

A sale is a dynamic, ever-changing relationship. Stay in close touch with the customer through all of it. The customer who invests in your solution today will be the customer who invests with you tomorrow, or the customer who puts in a good word on your behalf to a colleague. After your solution has been installed, follow up with some type of customer satisfaction report. Even if your marks are high, don't make the mistake of assuming that's the end of the story.

When is an order a *real* order? As we said, the superstar knows that it's not when the customer signs on the dotted line, it's not when you see the down payment, it's not when you have been paid your commission, and it's not even after the solution is delivered and installed. An order is an order only when you have a satisfied customer who actively recommends your solution to others — *and* becomes a repeat customer.

So stay in touch with your customers. Show up with your wits, your strategic thinking, your savvy, your good will, and most of all, your integrity — and watch the magic happen.

Close 'em!

Summary of Superstar Secrets

► Don't sell. Consult!

► Superstar sales is not about selling. It's about helping people buy.

► People don't buy products or services or features or benefits. They buy solutions to their problems and pain.

► The product doesn't matter. Most products or services will do the job. *You* matter.

► Go above and beyond. Provide assistance way beyond your product or service so that customers recognize you as a true consultant in your field.

► Imagine for a moment that the customer is your mother. Doesn't that immediately shift your attitude into ultra-empathy mode?

► Buyers who might not choose you for a friend will buy from you if they trust and respect you.

► You fall down so you can learn how to get up.

► Never lose twice for the same reason.

► As a starting point, treat customers the way you would like to be treated. Then follow my Modified Golden Rule: Treat customers the way *they* would like to be treated.

► Superstars differentiate themselves not by what they sell but by *how* they sell.

► Buyer decisions are made emotionally and then justified rationally.

► The one word that encompasses what it takes to truly become a superstar is *trust.* Trust is confidence that the other person has your best interests in mind.

► Nobody cares how much you know until they know how much you care. — *Theodore Roosevelt*

► Gain initial trust by researching your customer, asking powerful questions, providing non-solution-specific information, and telling success stories.

► The rep who develops, documents, and drives the customer's buying process... wins!

► You cannot influence what you do not know.

► Keep an eye out for STPs — superstar turning points. These are chances for you to stop and think, and then choose to be a consultant.

► Provide templates to help the customer document every stage of the buying process.

► Your value proposition should provide a clear, compelling answer to the question, "Why should I buy from you?"

Summary of Superstar Secrets (continued)

▶ Never criticize the competition. Instead, discuss the trade-offs of the various options available to the customer.

▶ The conversation is not about you! It's about the customer's needs.

▶ Don't waste scarce resources on dead-end prospects. Qualify quickly!

▶ The number one credibility tool is a blank sheet of paper.

▶ Don't let the customer define the path ahead. Define it yourself using this philosophy: My field! My time! My game! My rules!

▶ Never fight or argue with a customer. That would be like stepping in front of a speeding train.

▶ Use customer quotes in your slide presentations. People love seeing their ideas broadcast in bright lights.

▶ When making a presentation, you always, always, *always* want to go last.

▶ The goal in pricing is to position yourself as a consultant in the quote process and delay providing formal pricing as long as possible.

▶ Adopt the mindset that you will *never* quote.

▶ Sell value by highlighting the hard-dollar impact of your solution's unique unfair advantages.

▶ A customer objection is a gift handed to you on a silver platter — the chance to differentiate yourself as a superstar.

▶ An order is an order only after you have a satisfied customer, who actively recommends your solution to others — and becomes a repeat customer.

Top 18 Sales Rep Mistakes

Here's how to fail at high-end sales:

1 Come on strong.

2 Talk more than you listen.

3 Try to impress the customer with your technical prowess.

4 Dump data on your customer immediately.

5 Focus on winning the deal instead of helping the customer succeed.

6 Focus on product features instead of positively influencing your customer's financial health.

7 Focus on beating the competition instead of helping the customer invest in an appropriate solution.

8 Focus on selling instead of on helping people buy.

9 Begin negotiations too early.

10 Fail to plan for each sales call.

11 Provide pricing early.

12 Offer a solution before the customer trusts you.

13 Blurt out your spiel before you understand the customer's challenges and needs.

14 Refuse to discuss your solution's weaknesses or the competition's strengths.

15 Drag lots of brochures along on your sales calls.

16 Focus on your selling process instead of your customer's buying process.

17 Criticize the competition.

18 Instead of preparing in advance, kill with questions.

INDEX

ABOUT THE AUTHOR

Daniel J. Adams is the founder of Adams & Associates, which provides sales training and marketing strategy consulting to *Fortune* 100 firms. After a successful sales career with General Electric Healthcare, Cisco Systems, and Ariba, Inc., Dan developed Trust Triangle Selling™ – his interactive, best-practice-based approach to coaching sales teams, who appreciate his passion for teaching and commitment to their success. Dan has trained tens of thousands of sales executives in workshops across the country. He also provides private coaching to sales reps, sales managers, marketing executives, and business development executives.

Dan, who received an MBA from the University of Wisconsin, consults from his offices in Chicago, Illinois, and Bonita Springs, Florida.

◆

Contact us at our main office:

Adams & Associates
532 Walker Road
Hinsdale, Illinois 60521-3527
info@trusttriangleselling.com

Please include your name, title, company name, and phone number.

CPSIA information can be obtained at www.ICGtesting.com
Printed in the USA
LVOW100626260312

274718LV00001B/3/A